HOMEWORK
Helpster™

learn faster
grade **5**
score higher

Makes Homework Happen

Have you forgotten a lesson?

Can't remember a math formula?

Do you need to double-check your facts?

Now it's simple and easy

Just use the dividers to quickly find the a[...]

Each page takes you to a different lesson on a different to[...]

Each page summarizes lessons with examples and facts you need to know.

Available in the Series

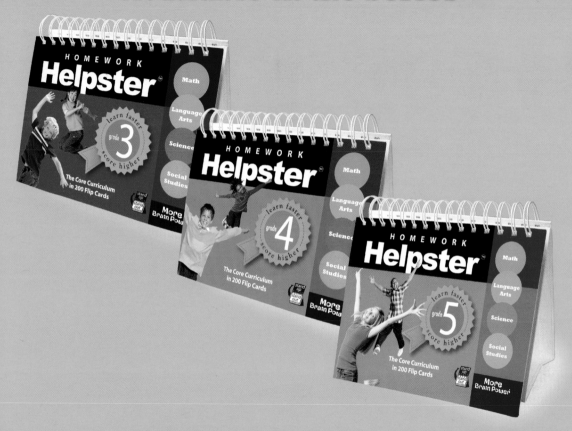

How to use your
H O M E W O R K
Helpster™

Chapter

Lesson

Unique Design
Stands up! Stands out!
At home or on the go!

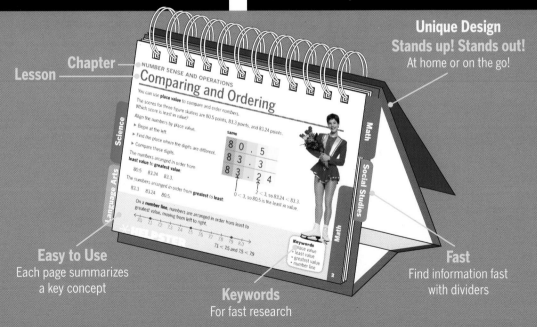

Easy to Use
Each page summarizes
a key concept

Keywords
For fast research

Fast
Find information fast
with dividers

TimeLine™

Notes

Social Studies Contents

The Granger Collection, New York

Sound

Science

Sound is a form of mechanical energy. In order for something to make a sound, it must be vibrating, or moving back and forth rapidly. Sound travels from one place to another by **waves.** Sound waves have two parts to them:

▶ The loudness or **volume** of a sound is controlled by the **amplitude** of the wave. The amplitude is a measure of how big a wave is and how much energy it has. The bigger the amplitude of the sound wave, the louder the sound.

▶ The **tone** or **pitch** of a sound is controlled by the **wavelength** and its **frequency.** Frequency is a measure of how fast a wave is vibrating. The faster the vibration, the higher the frequency and the shorter the length of the wave. High-frequency waves have short wavelengths and produce high-pitched sounds.

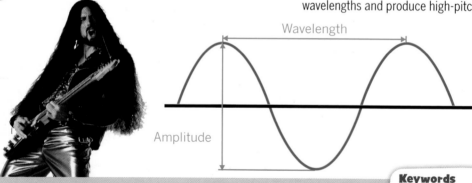

Wavelength

Amplitude

Unlike a light wave, which can travel through the vacuum of space, a sound wave must travel through some form of matter. Sound travels faster in solids, such as rock and steel, than in air or water.

Keywords
- sound
- waves
- volume
- amplitude
- tone
- pitch
- wavelength
- frequency

✳**HELPSTER**

Social Studies Contents (continued)

PHYSICAL SCIENCE
Magnetism

Magnetism is a force that can either **attract** or **repel.**
Magnetism happens in only certain metals, including iron,
steel, and cobalt. Electricity flowing through a circuit also
can produce a **magnetic field.**

A **permanent magnet** has two different poles
that are always set the same way. If the same
poles of two different magnets are brought near
each other, they will push away, or repel. If the
opposite poles of two magnets are brought near
each other, they will attract.

A **temporary magnet** can be switched on and off
and is made by an electric current flowing through
a conductor, such as a metal wire. These are called
electromagnets. Reversing the direction of the current flows
in the conductor reverses the poles of the electromagnet.
Turning off the current stops the magnetism.

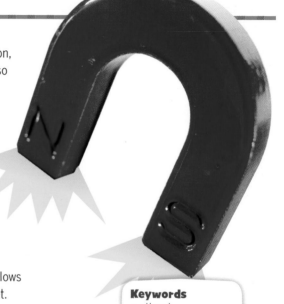

The force of a magnet is strongest at its poles. **Magnetic force** refers to
how far a magnet can pull objects near it. Magnetic fields spread out into
the space around a magnet, attracting iron and some other metals.

Keywords
- attract
- repel
- magnetic field
- permanent magnet
- temporary magnet
- electromagnets
- magnetic force

Social Studies **Keywords**

PHYSICAL SCIENCE
Electricity

Electricity is one of the most useful forms of energy to humans. It can light a light, create sound, produce heat, and make motors run. In order for electricity to work, it must flow through a **circuit.**

Circuits are closed pathways of **conductors** through which electricity can flow. A circuit can have any shape, but most circuits come in two main forms.

▶ **Series circuits** have the conductors lined up in a single pathway for electricity to flow. Any break in a series circuit will stop the electricity, and all the parts of the circuit will fail.

▶ **Parallel circuits** have two or more pathways of conductors that are side by side. If a component in one part of the circuit fails, the electricity has another "parallel" path to follow so the rest of the circuit remains active.

Most circuits in houses are of a parallel design. If a light burns out in one room, the rest of the lights in the house stay on. Some holiday lights are series circuits. If one bulb burns out, they all go out.

Keywords
- electricity
- circuit
- conductors
- series circuits
- parallel circuits

Social Studies Keywords (continued)

Reflection and Refraction

Science

Light is energy that interacts with matter in several different ways. It can be transmitted through clear objects. It can be absorbed by opaque objects. It can also be reflected and refracted.

Reflection happens when light strikes an object and bounces off. In a mirror, all the light rays that strike the surface bounce off in the same direction producing a reflected image. Mirrors are used to see objects behind you and around corners.

Refraction happens when light bends as it enters and leaves a transparent material at an angle. A **lens** is a curved piece of glass or plastic that is thicker at one part than another. As the light rays bend through the lens, they make an object appear bigger or smaller. A telescope, eyeglasses, and your eye all have lenses in them.

Reflection and refraction of light don't just happen in solid mirrors and lenses. Water can also bounce and bend light.

Keywords
- reflection
- refraction
- lens

HELPSTER

Reading a U.S. Physical Map

Relief Map of the United States

A **physical map** describes the landforms, bodies of water, and other natural features of a region. Some physical maps are **relief maps** that use color keys and shading to indicate higher and lower elevations. Others are **land-use maps** that show physical features such as farmland and the location of natural resources.

Legend—explains the symbols used on the map.

Compass rose—shows the cardinal directions (north, south, east, and west). Usually, the arrow points north.

Keywords
- physical map
- relief maps
- land-use maps

Social Studies

PHYSICAL SCIENCE
Energy

Energy makes matter move and comes in two main forms. When matter is put in motion, it is using **kinetic energy. Potential energy** is energy that has been stored and is waiting to be used.

Electrical potential energy stored in a battery is changed into light energy.

Chemical potential energy stored in the wood is changed to heat and light energy.

Gravitational potential energy stored in the train at the top of a hill is turned into kinetic energy as the cars roll down the slope.

Light energy from the sun is stored in plants as potential chemical energy.

Food is potential chemical energy. When it is digested, it fuels our bodies and keeps us moving.

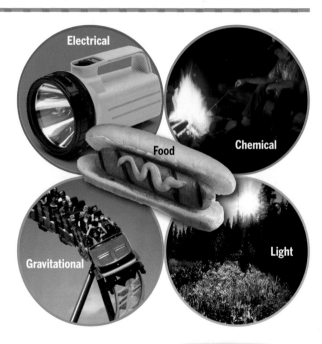

Keywords
- kinetic energy
- potential energy

41

Reading a U.S. Climate Map

Climate describes a region's **weather** (temperature and **precipitation**) over a long period of time. A **climate map** uses a color key to define different climate regions.

Climate zones affect the food people grow, the ways they dress, and the shelters they build. Latitude (distance from the equator), elevation, winds, oceans, and mountains control an area's climate.

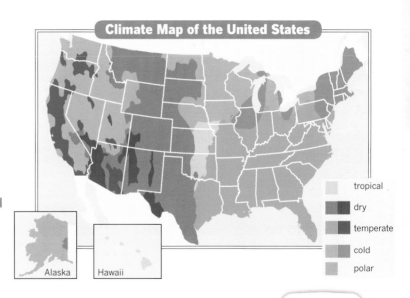

Climate Map of the United States

Alaska

Hawaii

- tropical
- dry
- temperate
- cold
- polar

Social Studies

Keywords
- climate
- weather
- precipitation
- climate map

PHYSICAL SCIENCE
Simple Machines

Simple machines help get **work** done by reducing the amount of **effort** needed to make something move. The trade-off is that you must move the object a greater distance. There are six simple machines.

▶ **Lever:** A bar that turns around a fixed point called a **fulcrum**.

▶ **Wheel and Axle:** A circular lever that turns around a central shaft.

▶ **Pulley:** A wheel and axle with a rope or chain on it.

▶ **Inclined Plane:** A ramp used for raising and lowering objects. Changing the slope of a ramp makes it easier or harder to move up it. The gentler the slope, the easier it is.

▶ **Screw:** A circular ramp curled around a central post.

▶ **Wedge:** An inclined plane on its side, used for cutting or splitting.

Screws

Pulley

Keywords
- simple machines
- work
- effort
- lever
- fulcrum
- wheel and axle
- pulley
- inclined plane
- screw
- wedge

Simple machines have few moving parts. Compound machines are made by putting together different simple machines.

*HELPSTER

Reading a U.S. Demographic Map

A **demographic map** describes information related to population, such as where people live or what work they do. In the year 2006, the population of the United States reached 300 million. Urban areas (cities) were the areas of the highest population. New York, Los Angeles, Chicago, Houston, and Philadelphia were the largest American cities. This map shows the density of population throughout the nation.

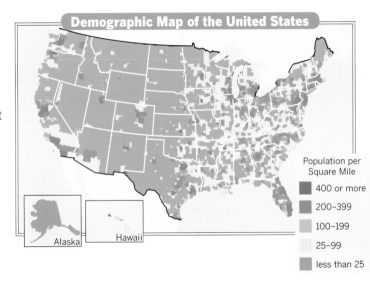

Demographic Map of the United States

Alaska   Hawaii

Population per Square Mile

- 400 or more
- 200–399
- 100–199
- 25–99
- less than 25

Social Studies

Every 10 years, the U.S. government counts the population by doing a **census**. In 1790, Secretary of State **Thomas Jefferson** conducted the first U.S. census. U.S. marshals on horseback counted 3.9 million people living in the young nation.

Keywords
- demographic map
- census
- Thomas Jefferson

3

Gravity

Science

Gravity is a **force** of attraction, pulling objects toward each other. The more **mass** an object has, the greater its gravitational force. On Earth, gravity pulls everything down toward the center of the planet.

Gravity controls how much an object weighs. **Weight** is the mass of an object times the force of gravity. Your weight would change on different planets in the solar system because each planet has a different mass and a different pull of gravity. This chart shows you what your weight would be on other planets if you weighed 100 pounds on Earth.

Weight of a 100-Pound Person on Other Planets

Planet	Weight	Planet	Weight
Mercury	38	Saturn	107
Venus	88	Uranus	90
Mars	38	Neptune	110
Jupiter	240		

Source: NASA

The sun has so much mass that its gravity is strong enough to hold the entire solar system together.

Keywords
- gravity
- force
- mass
- weight

HELPSTER

GEOGRAPHY
Reading a U.S. Political Map

A **political map** shows the boundaries of regions controlled by different governments and the names and locations of capitals and other major cities. This is a political map of the United States. Because the states of Alaska and Hawaii are not part of the continental United States, they are shown on **insets**.

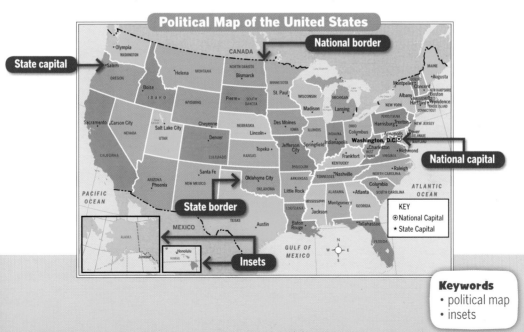

Keywords
• political map
• insets

4

PHYSICAL SCIENCE
Force and Motion

A **force** is any push or pull that makes an object move. In order to get something to move, you must overcome the force of **friction.** Friction is a force of resistance that pushes against things.

Friction happens when two moving objects rub against each other. The rougher the surface, the more friction there is. By making a surface smoother, you can reduce friction and make it easier to get work done. Waxing the bottom of skis and sharpening the blades of ice skates reduce friction, making them glide faster.

Friction can happen between two solid objects, or it can happen between a fluid and a solid. Air or water rubbing against a surface also creates a type of friction called **drag.** Boats and airplanes have smooth and pointed surfaces in order to reduce drag, making it easier for them to move.

Workers at an ice skating rink use a Zamboni® machine to smooth the ice and reduce friction, making it easier for people to skate.

Keywords
- force
- friction
- drag

The U.S. Constitution

The **Constitution** of the United States was ratified, or adopted, in 1788. This document lays out the laws that organize this country. It sets up the U.S. government as a republic and gives people and states important rights.

▶ The Preamble, or introduction, lists the goals of the government, which include justice, tranquillity (peace), self-defense, and liberty (freedom).

▶ The seven Articles describe the three branches of government and the relationships among the different states. They also explain how to make changes to the Constitution.

▶ The 27 Amendments are changes made to the Constitution after it was ratified. The first 10, which make up the **Bill of Rights**, give Americans the right to free speech, to choose their own religions, and to a free, uncensored press. The Bill of Rights also protects people accused of crimes and gives power to the states.

Amendments to the Constitution made slavery illegal (the 13th Amendment) and gave African-Americans (the 15th Amendment) and women (the 19th Amendment) the right to vote. Only the 18th Amendment (on prohibition) has been repealed.

Keywords
• Constitution
• Bill of Rights

Social Studies

PHYSICAL SCIENCE
Systems

In science, the term *system* means something that has a number of different parts all working together in a common way. Systems can take many forms and can be open or closed.

▶ **Open systems** can have new input from the outside. A pond is an example of an open **ecosystem** because it gets things like oxygen, carbon dioxide, and water from the atmosphere. The electrical circuits in your house are open energy systems because they get their power from outside.

▶ **Closed systems** get no new input from the outside. A **circuit** made from a lightbulb and a battery (as in a flashlight) is a closed energy system because once the battery runs out, the system stops. A sealed terrarium is an example of a closed ecosystem.

The earth is an open system because it is powered by the sun. The sun and the rest of the planets together make up a closed solar system.

Keywords
- open systems
- ecosystem
- closed systems
- circuit

Three Branches of Government

The Constitution organizes the U.S. government into three branches that balance each other's powers.

The **executive branch** (the president) leads the armed forces; makes treaties with other countries; appoints ambassadors, cabinet members, and federal judges; pardons criminals; and has the power to veto laws.

The **legislative branch** (the two houses of Congress: the Senate and the House of Representatives) makes laws, controls trade with other countries, must approve treaties, and can impeach the president and override his or her vetoes.

The **judicial branch** (the Supreme Court and lower federal courts) decides whether laws and treaties follow the Constitution and settles cases involving federal laws or controversies between two or more states.

Each state, city, or town has its own government. Governors and mayors make up the executive branch. State legislatures and city councils make laws. State or municipal courts ensure that the laws follow the state constitution or local regulations and that citizens follow the laws.

Keywords
- executive branch
- legislative branch
- judicial branch

Social Studies

✳HELPSTER

6

PHYSICAL SCIENCE
Chemical Changes

Chemical changes happen when atoms in matter get rearranged and new substances are formed. The new substances, or products, often have different properties than the original materials, or **reactants.** Some common chemical changes are:

▶ **Oxidation:** When something burns, carbon atoms combine with oxygen to form **carbon dioxide.** When metal rusts, oxidation also takes place as the iron reacts with oxygen in the air, producing iron oxide.

▶ **Fermentation:** When food ferments, tiny fungi called yeast cause the sugars in it to react to form carbon dioxide gas and alcohol.

▶ **Photosynthesis:** When plants photosynthesize, they use light energy to combine water and carbon dioxide and make simple sugars.

▶ **Digestion:** When we eat food, chemicals such as starch and protein are broken down into smaller products, which are used as fuel for the cells of our bodies.

Every time we cook food, a chemical change takes place. Chemical changes cannot be reversed.

Keywords
- chemical changes
- reactants
- oxidation
- carbon dioxide
- fermentation
- photosynthesis
- digestion

*HELPSTER

Making Laws

Laws help organize communities, describing important rights and responsibilities of citizens, businesses, and government officials. Federal laws are proposed as **bills** in Congress and signed into law by the president. Here are the basic steps in how a bill becomes a law.

▶ Bills can be introduced by senators in the Senate or representatives in the House.

▶ Once a bill is introduced, it is sent to a committee that specializes in the subject of the bill. The committee gathers information and sometimes makes changes to the bill before sending it back to the full House or Senate.

▶ After the bill is passed in the house where it was introduced, it is sent to the other house. The second house might have a different version of the bill in the works. In that case, the House and Senate compromise to come up with a version both houses can pass.

▶ Once both houses of Congress have approved the bill, it heads to the president. The president can sign the bill into law. Or he or she can **veto** it and send it back to Congress.

▶ Congress can override the veto by a two-thirds majority vote in the House and Senate. If that happens, the bill is sent back to the president.

▶ Now the president either signs the bill into law or does nothing. If he or she does nothing, the bill automatically becomes law after 10 days.

During the period from 1947 through 2000, the House introduced an average of 11,673 bills per two-year session. The Senate introduced an average of 3,808 bills per two-year session.

Keywords
• laws
• bills
• veto

Social Studies

7

PHYSICAL SCIENCE
Physical Changes

A **physical change** happens when the size, shape, or state of matter changes, but its composition stays the same. Physical changes usually can be reversed. Common physical changes include:

▶ **Crushing/Breaking:** If you crush a rock with a hammer or break a glass, the pieces are just smaller bits of the same material.

▶ **Melting/Freezing:** When matter changes from a liquid to a solid, it freezes. When it changes from a solid to a liquid, it melts. Either way, it's the same matter. This happens with ice, wax, and lava flowing out of a volcano.

▶ **Evaporating/Condensing:** When water boils, some of it evaporates and turns into a gaseous vapor. As the vapor cools, it will condense back to a liquid again. The two processes are opposites of each other and they can reverse as often as conditions will allow.

Most physical changes happen because of a change in energy. Heating, cooling, or squeezing a substance can cause a physical change.

Keywords
• physical change
• condense

The U.S. Presidents

The **president** of the United States leads the executive branch of the government. Presidents are elected every four years. Citizens age 18 and over are allowed to register to vote in a presidential election.

	President	Years in Office	Where Born
1	George Washington	1789–1797	Virginia
2	John Adams	1797–1801	Massachusetts
3	Thomas Jefferson	1801–1809	Virginia
4	James Madison	1809–1817	Virginia
5	James Monroe	1817–1825	Virginia
6	John Quincy Adams	1825–1829	Massachusetts
7	Andrew Jackson	1829–1837	South Carolina
8	Martin Van Buren	1837–1841	New York
9	William Henry Harrison	1841	Virginia
10	John Tyler	1841–1845	Virginia
11	James K. Polk	1845–1849	North Carolina
12	Zachary Taylor	1849–1850	Virginia
13	Millard Fillmore	1850–1853	New York
14	Franklin Pierce	1853–1857	New Hampshire
15	James Buchanan	1857–1861	Pennsylvania
16	Abraham Lincoln	1861–1865	Kentucky
17	Andrew Johnson	1865–1869	North Carolina
18	Ulysses S. Grant	1869–1877	Ohio
19	Rutherford B. Hayes	1877–1881	Ohio
20	James A. Garfield	1881	Ohio
21	Chester A. Arthur	1881–1885	Vermont

George Washington

PHYSICAL SCIENCE
Metals

One special group of chemical elements is called **metals**. While each individual metal has its own unique properties, all metals as a group share the following characteristics:

▶ **Strength:** Many metals are strong. Bridges made of steel are stronger than those made of wood.

▶ **Electrical Conductivity:** Most metals allow an electrical current to flow through them with little resistance. Copper is used for making wires, and the circuits in the space shuttle are gold-plated.

▶ **Thermal Conductivity:** Most metals are good conductors of heat and cold. Drinks stored in aluminum cans chill fast, and pots and pans made out of iron and steel heat up quickly.

▶ **Malleability:** Many metals are malleable, which means that they can be shaped and bent easily. Gold and silver are used to make jewelry because they are easy to mold and shape.

Steel bridge

Iron frying pan

Some metals, such as copper, are pure elements, while others such as brass and bronze are **alloys**, made from two or more different metals mixed together. Brass is made from copper and zinc. Bronze is made from copper and other elements, including tin.

Keywords
- metals
- conductivity
- malleability
- alloys

✳HELPSTER

34

The U.S. Presidents (continued)

	President	Years in Office	Where Born
22	Grover Cleveland	1885–1889	New Jersey
23	Benjamin Harrison	1889–1893	Ohio
24	Grover Cleveland	1893–1897	New Jersey
25	William McKinley	1897–1901	Ohio
26	Theodore Roosevelt	1901–1909	New York
27	William Howard Taft	1909–1913	Ohio
28	Woodrow Wilson	1913–1921	Virginia
29	Warren G. Harding	1921–1923	Ohio
30	Calvin Coolidge	1923–1929	Vermont
31	Herbert C. Hoover	1929–1933	Iowa
32	Franklin D. Roosevelt	1933–1945	New York
33	Harry S Truman	1945–1953	Missouri
34	Dwight D. Eisenhower	1953–1961	Texas
35	John F. Kennedy	1961–1963	Massachusetts
36	Lyndon B. Johnson	1963–1969	Texas
37	Richard M. Nixon	1969–1974	California
38	Gerald R. Ford	1974–1977	Nebraska
39	James E. Carter, Jr.	1977–1981	Georgia
40	Ronald W. Reagan	1981–1989	Illinois
41	George H. W. Bush	1989–1993	Massachusetts
42	William J. Clinton	1993–2001	Arkansas
43	George W. Bush	2001–	Connecticut

The White House

The 22nd Amendment to the Constitution, ratified in 1951, sets term limits for the president of the United States. It states: "No person shall be elected to the office of the President more than twice."

Keyword
• president

Social Studies

9

PHYSICAL SCIENCE
Molecules

Molecules are the "building blocks" of matter. Molecules form when atoms of different **elements** join together to form **compounds.**

Water is a typical compound. The water molecule is made up of two different elements, hydrogen and oxygen. The **chemical formula** for water is H_2O because each water molecule has one oxygen atom and two hydrogen atoms.

Sugar is a much more complex compound. Its chemical formula is $C_6H_{12}O_6$. Each sugar molecule has 6 carbon atoms, 12 hydrogen atoms, and 6 oxygen atoms.

Compounds usually have very different properties than the elements that make them. Water, for example, is made from hydrogen and oxygen, which are both gases that burn. But water is a liquid that can be used to put out fires!

Like words made from the letters of the alphabet, a small number of different atoms can be used to make millions of different molecules.

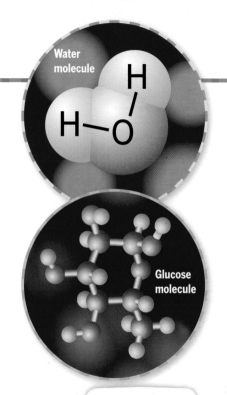

Water molecule

Glucose molecule

Keywords
- molecules
- elements
- compounds
- chemical formula

✳HELPSTER

33

GOVERNMENT
Citizenship

A citizen is a legal member of a nation. People born in the United States automatically acquire U.S. **citizenship**. Immigrants can become naturalized citizens if they fulfill certain requirements.

U.S. citizens have **rights**, including:

▶ the freedoms guaranteed by the U.S. Constitution;

▶ the right to vote (for those over 18);

▶ the right to hold certain government jobs (including president, for natural-born citizens); and

▶ a U.S. passport.

U.S. citizens also have **responsibilities**, including:

▶ learning about the issues and candidates, and voting;

▶ serving on a jury;

▶ supporting and defending the nation when called upon;

▶ obeying the laws of the nation;

▶ paying taxes; and

▶ respecting the rights of others.

Learn more about your state government and find out how to contact your representatives through your state's official Web site. Go to www.[state name].gov or www.state.[two-letter state postal abbreviation].us to be directed to the site.

Keywords
• citizenship
• rights
• responsibilities

Science

PHYSICAL SCIENCE
The Elements

Matter is made of individual units called **elements.** There are more than 100 different elements, each with its own set of properties. Scientists have organized them in a chart called the **periodic table.**

Each element on the periodic table has a different name, symbol, and **atomic number.**

Elements are made of tiny particles called **atoms,** which contain smaller **subatomic** particles called **protons.** Each element has a different number of protons.

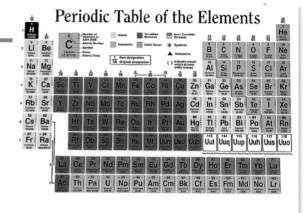

Periodic Table of the Elements

The simplest element is called hydrogen. Its atoms have only one proton, so it is the first element listed on the periodic table. It has an atomic number of 1. The atomic number is the number of protons an element's atoms have. For example, gold has an atomic number of 79 because it has 79 protons in one of its atoms.

Keywords
- elements
- periodic table
- atomic number
- atoms
- subatomic
- protons
- groups
- periods

The periodic table is divided into columns called **groups** and rows called **periods.** Elements that are listed in the same group have similar properties and behave in a similar fashion.

✳️HELPSTER

The Anthem and the Pledge

During the **War of 1812**, a very large American flag flew at Baltimore's Fort McHenry. After the British failed to capture that fort, Francis Scott Key wrote "The Star-Spangled Banner." His song became the **national anthem** of the United States in 1931. Most Americans memorize the first of its four verses:

Oh, say, can you see, by the dawn's early light,
What so proudly we hailed at the twilight's last gleaming?
Whose broad stripes and bright stars, through the perilous fight,
O'er the ramparts we watched, were so gallantly streaming?
And the rockets' red glare, the bombs bursting in air,
Gave proof through the night that our flag was still there.
Oh, say, does that star-spangled banner yet wave
O'er the land of the free and the home of the brave?

In 1892, Francis Bellamy wrote the original **Pledge of Allegiance** to celebrate the 400th anniversary of Christopher Columbus's voyage to America. Today Americans pledge:

I pledge allegiance to the Flag of the United States of America, and to
the Republic for which it stands, one Nation under God, indivisible,
with liberty and justice for all.

Social Studies

Keywords
- War of 1812
- national anthem
- Pledge of Allegiance

11

PHYSICAL SCIENCE
Matter

The term **matter** describes all the "stuff" found in the universe. Matter is made of tiny particles called **atoms**, has **mass** (weight), and takes up space. Matter takes four common forms called **states**:

▶ **Solid:** Keeps its shape unless energy acts on it. It's the most compact form of matter with the atoms close together, so solids usually have a high **density**.

▶ **Liquid:** Changes its shape to fit the container it's in. Liquids fill a container from the bottom up. The density of liquids varies quite a bit.

▶ **Gas:** Often invisible, can expand to fill an entire container. Gases have a very low density because their atoms are spread out.

▶ **Plasma:** Conducts electricity and glows. Plasmas are the most energetic form of matter. The sun is made of plasma, and so is lightning.

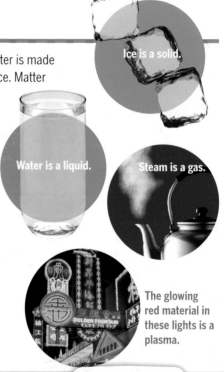

Ice is a solid.

Water is a liquid.

Steam is a gas.

The glowing red material in these lights is a plasma.

The law of conservation of matter says that matter cannot be created or destroyed, but it can be changed into energy.

Keywords
- matter
- atoms
- mass
- states
- density
- plasma

*HELPSTER

The First Americans

No one knows how long human beings have lived in the Americas. Today historians and archaeologists believe the first people reached the Americas as long as 20,000 years ago. Many **American Indians** say that their people have been here forever.

When Europeans arrived in the Americas 500 years ago, thousands of people lived here already. These **Native Americans** lived in groups, each a people who shared a language and ways of life. Those who lived within a geographical area often shared similar cultures.

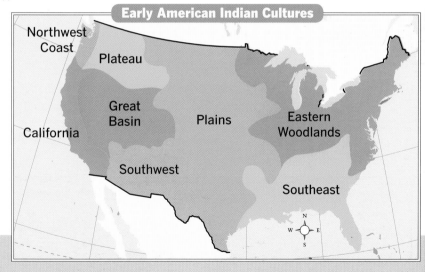

Early American Indian Cultures

Northwest Coast

Plateau

Great Basin

California

Plains

Eastern Woodlands

Southwest

Southeast

N W E S

Social Studies

Exploring Space

Since the development of rockets in the mid-1900s, people have had the ability to leave Earth and explore space. Spacecraft for exploration can be either **manned vehicles** or **unmanned probes.**

The first manned space flight was in 1961, when Yuri Gagarin became the first person to orbit the earth in a space capsule. Since that time, hundreds of astronauts have flown in space. In 1969, Neil Armstrong became the first person to walk on the moon.

Since the early 1960s, unmanned space probes have been sent to collect data on the moon, the sun, and other planets in our solar system. In the 1970s, *Voyager 2* flew past four planets, sending detailed pictures back to Earth, and the *Viking* space probes landed on Mars. Unmanned probes also have visited asteroids and comets.

Astronauts are currently living on the **International Space Station,** a permanent space base in orbit above Earth. They use the **space shuttle** to travel to and from Earth.

Lunar module on the moon

Keywords
- manned vehicles
- unmanned probes
- International Space Station
- space shuttle

*HELPSTER

The First Americans (continued)

Here are some features of life in each of the regions on the map of early American Indian cultures.

▶ **Northwest Coast:** A rich life focused on the sea • trade and fishing along rivers and the ocean • wooden houses, canoes, totem poles

▶ **California:** Hunter-gatherers in a bountiful environment • fishing along the coast • pole and brush houses, underground houses

▶ **Plateau:** Fishermen and hunters along large rivers • wooden frame lodges, earthen houses

▶ **Great Basin:** Hunter-gatherers in a harsh environment • pole houses covered with brush

▶ **Southwest:** Farmers in a dry land • adobe pueblos, animal skin and mud wickiups

▶ **Plains:** Hunters who moved with the buffalo • earthen lodges, tepees made of buffalo skins

▶ **Eastern Woodlands:** Farmers and hunters in the heavily wooded East • bark longhouses, wigwams, pit houses

▶ **Southeast:** Farmers and hunters • mud and bark houses with thatched roofs, log houses plastered with clay

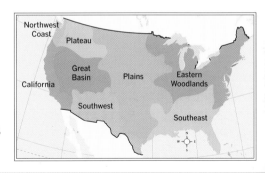

Columbus and the Spanish, who believed they had landed in the Indies, first called the native peoples Indians. Most native peoples use tribal names in their own languages, which often translate in English as "the people."

Keywords
• American Indians
• Native Americans

Social Studies

13

EARTH SCIENCE
Stargazing

Even though they look like dots in the sky, stars are really extremely hot balls of gas similar to the sun. They look much smaller because they are so far away. Different stars have different properties.

▶ **Brightness:** Stars have different degrees of brightness for different reasons. Some stars look bright because they are close to Earth. Other stars look bright because they are very large. Still other stars look bright because they are very hot.

▶ **Color:** Not all stars are white. They can be red, orange, yellow, or blue. The color of a star is related to its temperature. Blue stars are very hot, while red stars are cooler. Our sun appears to be yellow and is a medium-hot star.

▶ **Size:** Stars come in different sizes. Some are **red giants,** hundreds of times bigger then our sun. Some are **white dwarfs.** Our sun is a midsize star.

From Earth, stars appear to make shapes in the sky. These patterns are called **constellations.** They change with the seasons as Earth moves around the sun.

Keywords
• red giants
• white dwarfs
• constellations

Christopher Columbus

In the 1400s, European **explorers** began seeking faster ways to reach Asia, the source of spices and other items they valued. **Christopher Columbus** believed that Earth was a sphere and one could reach Asia by sailing west. In 1492, he convinced King Ferdinand and Queen Isabella of Spain to fund a westward voyage to Asia.

After sailing for two months, Columbus's ships reached land in October. Columbus thought he had reached Asia, but he had landed in what is now the Bahamas. He called the Taino people who lived there Indians. Columbus made three more voyages from Spain, but he never knew that he had reached the Americas, not Asia.

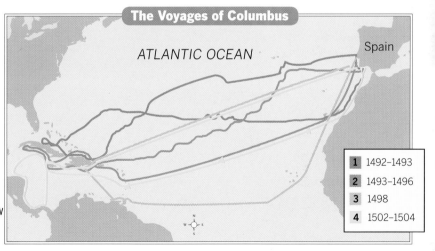

The Voyages of Columbus

ATLANTIC OCEAN

Spain

1	1492–1493
2	1493–1496
3	1498
4	1502–1504

Social Studies

Keywords
• explorers
• Christopher Columbus

14

EARTH SCIENCE
Orbits

An **orbit** is a predictable pathway that an object follows as it moves through space. Objects are held in their orbits by the force of **gravity.** Small objects orbit larger objects.

In our solar system, the sun has the most gravity, so **planets, asteroids,** and **comets** orbit it. Orbits are **ellipses,** or oval in shape.

The farther a planet is from the sun, the longer it takes to complete one orbit. Earth takes one year to complete one orbit. Neptune, the farthest planet from the sun, takes about 165 years!

Moons do not orbit the sun directly. Instead, they orbit their host planet. Every planet except Mercury and Venus has at least one moon orbiting it.

When our Moon orbits the earth, reflected light from the sun makes it appear to go through phases.

Keywords
- orbit
- gravity
- planets
- asteroids
- comets
- ellipses
- meteor shower

A **meteor shower** happens when Earth passes through the orbit of a comet that has traveled around the sun.

Exploring North America

The belief that Columbus had reached Asia by sailing west led other explorers to follow him. The next century became the **Age of Exploration** as Spain, France, the Netherlands, and England sponsored voyages to the Americas.

Spanish explorers seeking gold and conquests were known as **conquistadores**, or conquerors.

Explorer	Dates	Present–Day Area
Juan Ponce de León	1513	Puerto Rico, Florida
Hernán Cortés	1519–1521, 1532–1536	Mexico, California
Álvar Núñez Cabeza de Vaca	1528–1536	Mexico, New Mexico, Texas
Hernando de Soto	1539–1542	Southeastern United States
Francisco Vásquez de Coronado	1540–1542	Southwestern United States

French, Dutch, and English explorers searched for a Northwest Passage to Asia through North America.

Jacques Cartier	1534–1536	St. Lawrence River
Samuel de Champlain	1603–1616	Eastern Canada
Henry Hudson	1609	New York, Hudson River
	1610–1611	Canada, Hudson Bay

Amerigo Vespucci, who sailed for Spain, decided Columbus had reached another continent, not Asia. On a 1507 map, the "new" land was named America to honor him.

Keywords
- Age of Exploration
- conquistadores

Social Studies

15

EARTH SCIENCE
The Planets

There are eight known **planets** orbiting the **sun**. Recent discoveries suggest that there may be additional planets farther out in the **solar system**. Each of the planets is very different from the others.

Name	Diameter (kilometers)	Distance from Sun (kilometers)*	Composition
Mercury	4,879	57,909,175	Rock
Venus	12,104	108,208,930	Rock
Earth	12,756	149,597,890	Rock
Mars	6,787	227,936,640	Rock
Jupiter	142,800	778,412,020	Gas
Saturn	120,660	1,426,725,400	Gas
Uranus	51,118	2,870,972,200	Gas
Neptune	49,528	4,498,252,900	Gas

Source: NASA

*Distances from the sun vary during the planets' orbits.

The word planet is based on an ancient Greek word meaning "wanderer." In ancient times, people noticed that planets seemed to move back and forth across the sky, while the stars stayed fixed in their positions.

Keywords
- planets
- sun
- solar system

Europe Claims the Americas

In time, European **settlers** established **colonies** in North America. They came to find wealth, religious freedom, and new opportunities. By the early 1700s, much of North America was divided among the British, French, and Spanish.

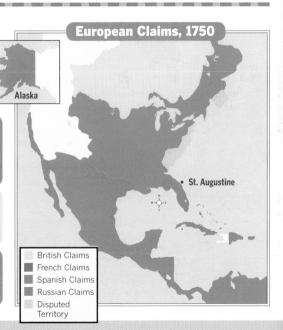

European Claims, 1750

Alaska

• St. Augustine

British Claims
French Claims
Spanish Claims
Russian Claims
Disputed Territory

Trade, mainly in furs, was the basis for New France.

St. Augustine (founded by the Spanish in 1565) was the first permanent European settlement in what is now the United States.

After exploration by Russia in 1728, fur traders claimed parts of what is now Alaska.

Between 1607 and 1732, the British settled or took over 13 colonies in what is now the United States.

In New Spain, soldiers built presidios (forts) and priests set up missions.

What about the Dutch and the Swedes? Between 1625 and 1664, both had colonies in what are now New York and New Jersey. They were taken over by the British in 1664.

Keywords
• settlers
• colonies

Social Studies

HELPSTER

16

EARTH SCIENCE
The Sun

The sun is a medium-sized star producing heat and light by a process called **nuclear fusion.** It is the only star in our solar system. It is located at the center, with the planets orbiting around it.

THE SUN

Size	About 864,000 miles (1,400,000 kilometers) in diameter or 109 times greater than the width of the earth. One million Earths could fit inside the volume of the sun.
Mass	99 percent of the solar system's mass is in the sun.
Temperature	The outer surface of the sun is about 10,000° Fahrenheit (5,500° Celsius). Scientists estimate that the interior temperature is more than 18,000,000° Fahrenheit (10,000,000° Celsius).
Composition	72 percent hydrogen, 26 percent helium, and 2 percent heavier elements. Hydrogen is constantly converted to helium by nuclear fusion reactions.
Atmosphere	The sun has three main layers. The part we see is the **photosphere.** Above this are the **chromosphere** and **corona.** On the photosphere, dark patches called **sunspots** appear and disappear.

Even though the sun is very hot, the gas in it is not burning like a fire. Its heat comes from a nuclear reaction, similar to what happens in a hydrogen bomb.

Keywords
- nuclear fusion
- photosphere
- chromosphere
- corona
- sunspots

The New England Colonies

In 1620, a group of English colonists heading for Virginia reached what is now Massachusetts. Settlers, who came to be called the **Pilgrims**, founded the Plymouth Colony. Within 60 years, there were four **New England colonies**.

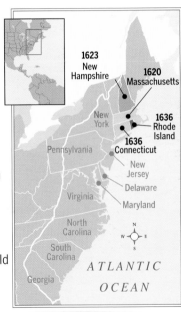

▶ The Pilgrims and the **Puritans**, who later settled Boston, set up communities based on strict religious practices.

▶ The founders of Connecticut wanted more freedom and financial opportunities.

▶ The founders of Rhode Island sought freedom of religion and separation of church and state.

▶ Settlers founded New Hampshire for trade, to sell lumber to England.

▶ Most New Englanders lived in small, self-sufficient towns where they raised their own food and had democratic town meetings, where all could participate.

▶ Boston, New England's leading city, was a center of trade with Britain.

The Mayflower Compact—signed by the Pilgrims on the *Mayflower*—established the first self-government in the colonies.

Keywords
- Pilgrims
- New England colonies
- Puritans

Social Studies

EARTH SCIENCE
Earth's Resources

We depend on many **nonrenewable resources** that are found below the surface of the earth. Most of these resources formed millions of years ago, and once they have been used, they are gone forever.

▶ **Coal:** Burned in factories and power plants for energy, releasing gases that pollute the air and cause global warming. Wind, solar power, and water power can be used instead of coal to make electricity.

▶ **Oil:** Used to make fuels for transportation and to heat buildings. It also releases gases that pollute the air and cause global warming when burned. Solar heating systems and fuels made from plants can be used instead of oil.

▶ **Metal Ores:** Buried in the earth and the source of copper, iron, and aluminum. Mining these ores requires a large amount of energy and creates many environmental problems. **Recycling** metal saves energy and reduces damage to the environment by reducing the need for more mining.

By conserving nonrenewable resources, recycling, and using more **renewable resources,** such as wind, sunlight, and water power, people will be able to power our society with fewer environmental problems.

Keywords
- nonrenewable resources
- recycling
- renewable resources

The Middle Colonies

From the beginning, the **Middle Colonies** were the most international of the 13 colonies. Dutch settlers founded New Netherland in 1625. Swedes settled in what became New Jersey and Delaware. English Quakers settled Pennsylvania.

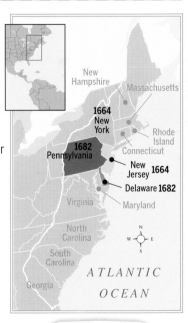

- ▶ In 1625, settlers sponsored by the Netherlands settled on Manhattan Island and the upriver area claimed by **Henry Hudson**. The goal was trade, especially in furs.

- ▶ In 1638, Swedes set up trading posts to the south, which were taken over by the Dutch in 1655.

- ▶ After the Duke of York captured New Netherland and New Sweden in 1664, they became the British colonies of New York and New Jersey.

- ▶ Quaker William Penn created a refuge for religious freedom in Pennsylvania.

- ▶ New York and Philadelphia were the major trading cities of the region.

- ▶ Rich farmland in the region produced so much grain that it was called the breadbasket of the colonies.

The name of heavily wooded Pennsylvania means "Penn's woods." **William Penn** received the grant for the colony from King Charles II of England.

Keywords
- Middle Colonies
- Henry Hudson
- William Penn

Social Studies

HELPSTER

18

Science

EARTH SCIENCE
Soil

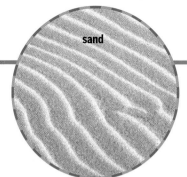

sand

Soil forms when **sediment** (pieces of worn rock) and decomposed plant material called **humus** mix on the earth's surface. Different soils have different properties, depending on the type of sediment they contain.

▶ **Sand:** Large particles about the size of sugar. Sandy soils drain very quickly and don't hold water. Nutrients quickly wash out of them.

▶ **Silt:** Medium-sized sediment that feels like flour. Soils rich in silt hold on to water and drain slowly. They are usually very fertile and are rich in nutrients.

▶ **Clay:** Microscopic-sized sediment that is sticky when wet and hard when dry. Clay soils drain very poorly, and plants have a hard time getting nutrients from them.

▶ **Loam:** A mixture of sand, silt, and clay-sized particles. It is the best soil for most plants, rich in nutrients and able to hold on to enough water to keep from drying out.

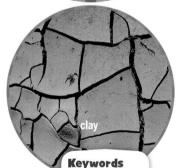

clay

Keywords
- sediment
- sand
- silt
- clay
- humus
- loam
- decomposers

Bacteria and other **decomposers** recycle nutrients by creating humus. Humus makes soil fertile. Without it, most plants wouldn't be able to grow.

The Southern Colonies

The British colonies began in Virginia when **Jamestown** was settled in 1607. Maryland and then the Carolinas came next. The last of the British colonies settled—Georgia—also is part of the **Southern Colonies**.

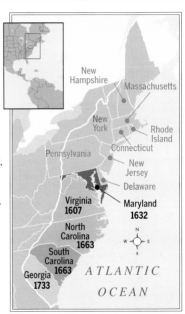

▶ The first Jamestown settlers came looking for gold. When that failed, they were saved by tobacco, which they sold to England.

▶ Maryland began in 1632 as a refuge for Catholics escaping unfair treatment in England.

▶ First settled in 1663, Carolina split into North and South Carolina in 1712. Rice was the area's cash crop.

▶ In 1733, the first settlers—debtors who were in prison for owing money—came to Georgia.

▶ Farming supported the region. The large farms, called **plantations**, needed large numbers of laborers. Many of those workers were enslaved Africans.

▶ Charleston, the region's leading city, was a wealthy trading center.

Virginia's House of Burgesses, founded in 1619, was the colonies' first governing body.

Keywords
- Jamestown
- Southern Colonies
- plantations

Social Studies

✳HELPSTER

EARTH SCIENCE
The Rock Cycle

There are more than a hundred different kinds of rocks found on Earth, which are constantly being recycled. Scientists place rocks into three different groups depending on how they form.

Igneous Rocks
Lava from volcanoes forms igneous rocks on the surface, and magma creates igneous rocks underground. Igneous rocks were all once hot liquid rock.

Sedimentary Rocks
The weathering of rock by wind, rain, and ice produces small pieces called sediment. Sediments are eroded by water and deposited in another place, where they get squeezed and cemented back together, forming a new rock.

Metamorphic Rocks
When rocks get buried deep in the earth, heat and pressure cause them to change. Metamorphic rocks form when minerals recrystallize without melting.

Sedimentary rocks

Sedimentary rocks such as salt and gypsum can also form as **crystals** when mineral-rich water evaporates.

Keywords
- igneous rocks
- sedimentary rocks
- metamorphic rocks
- crystals

✳HELPSTER

Slavery

Phillis Wheatley

Slavery was part of the colonial experience from the early days. African men, women, and children were kidnapped from their homes and sold into slavery. Although most slaves were in the south, enslaved Africans lived throughout the 13 colonies.

▶ The first Africans brought to the British colonies arrived in Jamestown in 1619. They may have been **indentured servants**, given their freedom after working without pay for several years.

▶ As the slave trade became a big business, millions of Africans were enslaved. Slaves kidnapped in Africa were brought by ship across the Atlantic. In this terrible **Middle Passage**, many died.

▶ In the South, slave labor made large plantations possible. In other colonies, most slaves worked in homes or businesses for the colonists who held them in bondage.

Part of the slave trade to the colonies was a **triangular trade**. Slaves and products such as molasses, lumber, guns, and rum were traded between West Africa, the West Indies, and New England.

Keywords
- slavery
- indentured servants
- Middle Passage
- triangular trade

Social Studies

✳ HELPSTER

20

EARTH SCIENCE
Inside the Earth

Even though Earth is made of rock, the planet is not a solid mass. Instead, it is made up of several different layers, some of which flow like super-thick liquids.

Inner Core: A solid mass of iron and nickel about 746 miles (1,200 kilometers) in diameter.

Crust: A layer of solid rock ranging from 6 to 40 miles (10 to 65 kilometers) thick and made up of several dozen pieces called **tectonic plates.** These plates move when the slow-moving currents in the mantle flow. When the moving plates rub against each other, they make earthquakes.

Outer Core: A layer of liquid iron and nickel about 1,398 miles (2,250 kilometers) thick. Movement of the liquid outer core around the solid inner core is thought to produce Earth's **magnetic field.**

Mantle: A layer of very dense semi-solid rock about 1,802 miles (2,900 kilometers) thick. Radioactive elements partially melt the rock, creating slow-moving currents.

Keywords
- crust
- tectonic plates
- mantle
- inner core
- outer core
- magnetic field
- plate tectonics

Plate tectonics is a scientific theory that explains how the outer surface of the earth changes due to the movement of rock under the surface. It explains why we have earthquakes, volcanoes, and mountains.

✳HELPSTER

The French and Indian War

Between 1754 and 1763, Great Britain and France were at war in North America. American Indians were the third party in the conflict, as different Native American nations sided with either Britain or France. The **French and Indian War** began over control of the Ohio River country and moved north.

War begins near Fort Duquesne (now Pittsburgh), where two rivers meet to form the Ohio River—a spot where both Britain and France want to build a fort. Young Major **George Washington** surrenders to the victorious French.

War moves north, as the British win an important victory at Louisbourg. They also take Fort Duquesne.

In the **Treaty of Paris**, France surrenders all claims in North America except for New Orleans and a few small islands in the West Indies.

1755

1759

1754

1758

1763

British General Edward Braddock and his army are defeated while trying to capture Fort Duquesne.

The British capture Fort Ticonderoga and Quebec.

How did this war get its name? The British-American forces named it after their enemies in the conflict: the French and the many American Indian nations who were their allies. In Europe, the conflict was part of what is called the **Seven Years' War**.

Keywords
- French and Indian War
- George Washington
- Treaty of Paris
- Seven Years' War

Social Studies

✳HELPSTER

EARTH SCIENCE
The Nitrogen Cycle

All living things need the chemical element nitrogen. While there is plenty of nitrogen on Earth, it must be changed before it can be used. These changes happen in the **nitrogen cycle.**

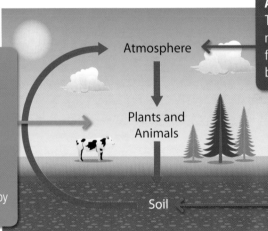

Atmosphere
The air is 78 percent nitrogen, but it is in a form that can't be used by most living things.

Plants and Animals
Nitrogen is found in all plant and animal cells. After it has been changed by bacteria, plants take nitrogen in through their roots. Animals get their nitrogen by eating plants or other animals. After living things die, nitrogen is released back to the soil and air by decomposing **bacteria.**

Atmosphere

Plants and Animals

Soil

Soil
In the soil, bacteria living on the roots of certain plants take nitrogen out of the air and chemically change it into a form that plants can use.

While most nitrogen is taken out of the air by bacteria, it also can be changed into a useable form by lightning when it strikes the ground.

Keywords
• nitrogen cycle
• bacteria

Declaring Independence

After the French and Indian War, colonists protested when Great Britain:

▶ expected them to help pay for the war,

▶ forbade them to move into lands once part of New France, and

▶ gave royal governors new powers.

Boston Tea Party

How the Colonists in America Protested

▶ The British Parliament passed new taxes on the colonists. Most troubling was the 1765 **Stamp Act**, which forced the colonists to buy a stamp for anything written or printed on paper.

▶ Above all, some American colonists protested taxation without representation. The colonies had no representatives in Parliament, which was passing taxes without their consent.

▶ Groups like the Sons of Liberty and the Daughters of Liberty urged the American colonists to boycott British goods.

How the Colonists in America United

▶ Some colonists took action in confrontations such as the 1770 **Boston Massacre**.

▶ The Committees of Correspondence organized protests such as the **Boston Tea Party**.

▶ At **Lexington** and **Concord** in 1775, colonial militia fired the first shots of war.

EARTH SCIENCE
The Carbon Cycle

Carbon is an important chemical element. It is part of every living thing. It's also found in the air, in oceans, and in rocks. The path that carbon takes through all these places is called the **carbon cycle.**

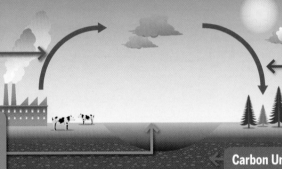

Living Carbon
During **photosynthesis, carbon dioxide** gas is taken from the air and turned into simple sugar by plants. It then becomes part of most cells. When living things die, carbon is released from their bodies by decomposers.

Atmospheric Carbon
Carbon dioxide gas enters the air when animals exhale and when we burn wood, coal, and other fuels.

Carbon in the Sea
Carbon dioxide is dissolved in ocean water, where it is used by sea creatures to make shells.

Carbon Underground
Many rocks, including limestone, marble, and coal, contain carbon.

Keywords
- carbon cycle
- photosynthesis
- carbon dioxide
- fossil fuels
- global warming

All **fossil fuels**, such as oil and coal, contain carbon that was once part of a living thing. When we burn them, carbon dioxide gas is released into the air. The extra carbon dioxide in the atmosphere contributes to **global warming**.

✳HELPSTER

How the Colonists in America Declared Independence

▶ **Thomas Paine** helped persuade colonists to cut ties with Britain in his pamphlet *Common Sense*.

▶ Delegates at the **Second Continental Congress** declared independence in 1776.

▶ In the **Declaration of Independence**, Thomas Jefferson explained
  • why the colonists had to break with Britain,
  • their goals for a new government, and
  • their grievances against Britain.

▶ Jefferson's words described the heart of the colonists' ideals: "We hold these truths to be self-evident, that all men are created equal, that they are endowed by their Creator with certain unalienable Rights, that among these are Life, Liberty and the pursuit of Happiness."

The Granger Collection, New York

Thomas Jefferson

Social Studies

Keywords
• Stamp Act
• Boston Massacre
• Boston Tea Party
• Lexington and Concord
• Thomas Paine
• Second Continental Congress
• Declaration of Independence

While many colonists protested, some colonists called Loyalists remained loyal to Britain and its king.

HELPSTER

EARTH SCIENCE
The Atmosphere

The **atmosphere** is like an ocean of air surrounding the earth. Just like water in the ocean, air also has pressure, which is measured with a **barometer.** The atmosphere has the following layers:

Thermosphere: The air here is so thin that pressure can barely be measured. The top of the atmosphere is about 373 miles (600 kilometers) above the earth. Beyond this is outer space.

Mesosphere: Starting at about 31 miles (50 kilometers) above the surface of the earth, it has a layer of electrically charged particles called the **ionosphere** near the top.

Stratosphere: Starting about 12 miles (20 kilometers) above the surface of the earth, it is thinner than the troposphere. The protective **ozone layer** is found here.

Troposphere: The layer closest to Earth where the air is the thickest and **air pressure** is the greatest. Daily weather changes in precipitation, temperature, and wind happen here.

Thermosphere

Mesosphere

Stratosphere

Troposphere

Wind happens when air moves from areas of high pressure to low pressure. The bigger the difference in air pressure, the faster the wind speed.

Keywords
- atmosphere
- barometer
- thermosphere
- mesosphere
- ionosphere
- stratosphere
- ozone layer
- troposphere
- air pressure

19

The American Revolution

From 1776 to the war's end in 1783, Americans—once 13 colonies, now 13 states—fought to become one nation. During the war, about a third of the colonists were **Patriots** supporting independence, a third were Loyalists, and a third were neutral.

- ▶ Led by General **George Washington**, the **Continental Army** lost in New York but won in New Jersey.

- ▶ A 1777 Continental victory at Saratoga was the turning point, bringing needed French support to the struggling new nation.

- ▶ After a winter of hardship at Valley Forge, the conflict spread west and south.

- ▶ Peace talks began soon after the British defeat at Yorktown in 1781. The 1783 Treaty of Paris ended the eight-year conflict. The United States had won its fight for independence.

Washington at Valley Forge

The Granger Collection, New York

Americans had help from many directions in the war. The Marquis de Lafayette (France), Tadeusz Kósciuszko and Kazimierz Pulaski (Poland), and Baron Friedrich von Steuben (Germany) came to help the Patriots.

Keywords
- Patriots
- George Washington
- Continental Army

Social Studies

HELPSTER

24

EARTH SCIENCE
Weather Maps

Weather maps provide a great deal of information on what the current weather conditions are. Knowing how to read the symbols on a weather map can help you predict how the weather will change.

High and **low pressure zones** show areas where high and low air pressure systems are. High pressure usually means fair weather; low pressure means a storm.

Cloud cover shows how cloudy it will be.

Precipitation shows whether it is raining, snowing, or clear. It also shows if severe weather, such as thunderstorms, is expected.

Temperature tells what the local high and low temperatures are expected to be for the day.

Fronts show where air masses of different temperatures meet. Fronts usually signal that precipitation will happen.

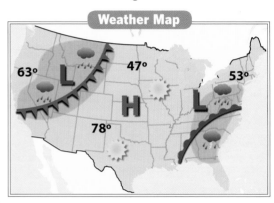

Weather Map

The **jet stream** is a fast-moving air current that flows from west to east around the earth, moving weather systems as it goes.

Keywords
- high pressure zone
- low pressure zone
- cloud cover
- precipitation
- temperature
- fronts
- jet stream

Writing the U.S. Constitution

When the Americans won the war and the 13 states were truly independent, they needed to make decisions about their government. As "united states," what kind of union would they have?

▶ In the **Articles of Confederation**, ratified in 1781, the states avoided a strong federal government. They created a republic (the people elected representatives to run the government) with a national legislature, but no national executive.

▶ Because states often disagreed, the country was seldom able to take action as a unified nation.

▶ In 1787, a Constitutional Convention met to draft a new plan of government. Delegates created a federal system, with powers shared by national and state governments.

▶ Conflicts between large and small states were settled in the Great Compromise, which established different rules for electing senators and representatives.

▶ After the **U.S. Constitution** was ratified, the new government went to work in 1789.

The nation's one great success under the Articles of Confederation was the **Northwest Ordinance**, passed in 1787. It set up a process for admitting western territories to the Union as new states.

Keywords
- Articles of Confederation
- U.S. Constitution
- Northwest Ordinance

EARTH SCIENCE
Weather Patterns

Weather conditions are always changing. Air temperature, barometric pressure, precipitation, wind speed, and wind direction change due to differences in the way energy flows through the atmosphere.

When the sun shines on Earth, the surface gets warm and heats the air above it. The warm air rises and cooler air flows in from the sides to replace it, producing wind. As the rising air moves away from the ground, it cools and begins to sink, forming a circular loop called a **convection cycle.**

Convection alone doesn't control the weather. Oceans affect weather patterns because they store a great deal of heat energy and add moisture to the air. Since water temperature is usually different than that of land, convection cycles over the ocean usually make the wind blow in a different direction.

During the day, breezes blow from the ocean toward the land. At night, breezes blow from the land toward the ocean.

Keyword
- convection cycle

The Louisiana Purchase

After the American Revolution, the United States stretched from the Atlantic to the Mississippi. Louisiana, the 800,000 square miles between the river and the Rocky Mountains, was claimed by Spain. In 1800, Spain secretly gave it to France.

President **Thomas Jefferson** dreamed of enlarging the nation so that it stretched from the Atlantic to the Pacific. He asked France to sell Louisiana to the United States. In 1803 they did—for $15 million. It was a bargain even then.

The **Louisiana Purchase** doubled the size of the United States, making it one of the world's largest countries. Jefferson sent **Meriwether Lewis** and **William Clark** on a journey of more than two years to explore some of the area.

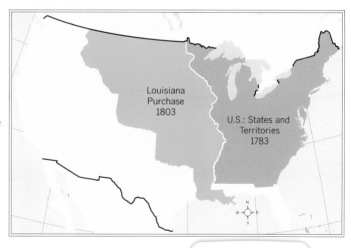

Louisiana
Purchase
1803

U.S.: States and
Territories
1783

Social Studies

Eventually, all or parts of 13 new states were created out of the land acquired through the Louisiana Purchase.

Keywords
• Thomas Jefferson
• Louisiana Purchase
• Meriwether Lewis
• William Clark

✻HELPSTER

26

EARTH SCIENCE
The Water Cycle

About three-quarters of the earth is covered by water, but most of it is salt water found in the oceans. Animals and plants need **freshwater,** which is produced by the **water cycle.** The water cycle has six parts.

Condensation
As water vapor cools, it turns back into liquid water and ice, forming clouds.

Precipitation
Water returns to the Earth's surface as either rain or snow.

Transpiration
Plants take up water from the soil and put it back into the air as water vapor.

Evaporation
Energy from the sun causes surface water to turn into freshwater vapor.

Runoff
Water that does not become groundwater flows into streams and rivers and is stored in ponds and lakes.

Groundwater
Water that seeps into the soil and moves underground to supply wells.

Keywords
- freshwater
- water cycle
- condensation
- evaporation
- groundwater
- precipitation
- transpiration
- runoff

Earth has very little "new" water. Most of our water has been here for billions of years and is constantly being recycled.

✴HELPSTER

The War of 1812

Conflict between Britain and the United States did not end in 1783. There was a second, and last, war between these two countries—the **War of 1812**.

▶ As settlers moved into the Northwest Territory, conflicts with American Indians were inevitable. The British became involved in these conflicts. Americans believed the British supplied guns to the Shawnee chief **Tecumseh**, who tried to unite Native Americans to protect their land.

▶ British ships began stopping American ships to prevent trade between the United States and Europe.

▶ Many Americans wanted to force the British to leave Canada. In 1812, Congress declared war on Britain.

▶ In 1813, Commodore Oliver Hazard Perry, commanding the U.S. Navy, defeated the British fleet on Lake Erie. The British lost control of the Great Lakes.

▶ In 1814, British troops burned the **White House** and the Capitol Building in Washington.

▶ Not realizing that peace had been declared, Americans won a victory in the Battle of New Orleans in 1815. ──────▶

Beginning in 1800, the new city of Washington, D.C., became the U.S. capital and the seat of federal government.

Keywords
• War of 1812
• Tecumseh
• White House

Social Studies

✳HELPSTER

LIFE SCIENCE
Disease

A **disease** is a condition that develops in the body, which causes it to work improperly and may even lead to death. While some are inherited, behavioral choices often contribute.

▶ **Diabetes** results in having too much sugar in the blood. It can lead to kidney failure. Diabetes is caused by the body not producing enough insulin. It can be controlled by insulin injections, and can often be avoided by eating low sugar foods and staying fit.

▶ **High blood pressure (hypertension)** is caused by clogged arteries, which make the push of blood through them a strain. It can lead to a **heart attack** or **stroke**, but can be treated by taking medicine. It can be avoided by getting exercise, not smoking, and eating foods low in salt.

▶ **Lung cancer** is the result of abnormal cell growth that forms **tumors** in the lungs, causing them to fail. It has many causes and has been linked to breathing polluted air and smoking. By not smoking, people reduce their risk of getting this disease.

Keywords
- disease
- diabetes
- hypertension
- heart attack
- stroke
- lung cancer
- tumors

By eating healthy foods and getting plenty of rest and exercise, you can reduce your risk of developing many diseases.

The Nation Moves West

After the Revolutionary War, pioneers pushed westward into the newly expanded United States. The **westward movement** was at its peak in the 1800s.

▶ Daniel Boone led pioneers across the Appalachian Mountains in the late 1700s.

▶ Improvements in transportation played a role. The **Erie Canal** opened in 1825. Steam engines powered boats and railroads to transport Americans west.

▶ In the 1840s, a tide of Americans followed the **Oregon Trail** to settle in the Pacific Northwest.

▶ Members of the Church of Jesus Christ of Latter-day Saints (Mormons) fled religious persecution to settle in the Utah Territory.

▶ People flooded California after gold was discovered there in 1848.

Westward Trails

- Daniel Boone
- Erie Canal
- Oregon Trail
- Mormon Trail
- California Trail

American Indians moved west, too, but against their will. In 1830, the **Indian Removal Act** enabled the president to force any Indians east of the Mississippi to move west.

Keywords
- westward movement
- Erie Canal
- Oregon Trail
- Indian Removal Act

Social Studies

LIFE SCIENCE
Nutrition

Understanding how different foods work in the body and how they promote good health, growth, and body development is what **nutrition** is all about. Foods contain several important substances.

Carbohydrates include sugars and starch. They provide energy and are found in things like bread, pasta, and potatoes.

Fats, including oils, also provide energy, but should be used in limited amounts. Fats are found in meat, nuts, and dairy products.

Proteins are important for building cells and are found in meat, eggs, beans, and milk.

Water is important because it is used in many different body systems.

Vitamins are found in fruits and vegetables and they help to control different body systems.

Minerals include calcium, which is important for building bones, and iron, which is important for red blood cells. Minerals come from a variety of foods, including green leafy vegetables.

Most packaged foods have a nutritional label on them that explains how much of each substance they contain.

Keywords
- nutrition
- carbohydrates
- fats
- proteins
- water
- vitamins
- minerals

The Missouri Compromise

Over time, 11 northern states abolished **slavery** within their borders. Slavery was legal in 11 southern states. As western territories applied for statehood, Congress faced a problem. Should slavery be legal in the new states? Northern free states said NO. Southern slave states said YES.

Henry Clay

▶ When a territory had a population of 60,000, it could apply for statehood. In 1819, the Missouri Territory applied to join the Union as a slave state. This would create a majority of slave states in Congress.

▶ Fierce arguments raged across the nation. Finally, Kentucky senator Henry Clay proposed a solution. His idea became known as the **Missouri Compromise**. The plan was to allow Missouri to become a slave state and the new state of Maine to become a free state. Future states north of an imaginary line would be free states and south of the line would be slave states.

▶ The plan worked for 30 years: Three new slave states and three new free states came into the Union.

Henry Clay later came up with the **Compromise of 1850**. This allowed California in as a free state. Voters in New Mexico and Utah were to decide whether to be free or slave states.

Keywords
• slavery
• Missouri Compromise
• Compromise of 1850

Social Studies

LIFE SCIENCE
Reproduction

Reproduction is an important part of life. Without it, there would be no new living things to take the place of individual plants and animals that die. Reproduction happens in two different ways.

▶ **Asexual reproduction** happens when a new living thing grows directly from a single parent and is common in plants and some animals. A new plant growing from the stem of a plant that has been cut is an example of asexual reproduction.

▶ **Sexual reproduction** happens when a male cell **(sperm)** from one individual joins up with and **fertilizes** a female cell **(egg)** from another individual. Once fertilization takes place, the new cells quickly start to grow and divide, producing an **embryo.** If conditions are right, the embryo will eventually grow to become a new adult, with genetic information and characteristics from both parents in its cells.

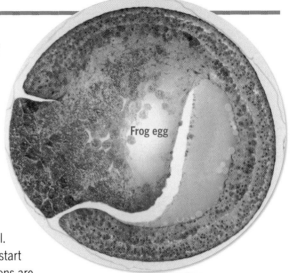

Frog egg

For humans, it takes about nine months from the time an egg is fertilized for a new embryo to grow enough to be born.

Keywords
- reproduction
- asexual reproduction
- sexual reproduction
- sperm
- fertilizes
- egg
- embryo

Texas Independence

First part of New Spain, Texas became part of Mexico in 1821 when Mexico won its independence. Soon the Mexican government put a stop to the small American colony **Stephen F. Austin** had begun in Texas. From there, the situation got worse.

▶ Trouble began when Mexican dictator General **Antonio López de Santa Anna** sent troops to force Texans to obey Mexican laws.

▶ In 1835, Texans attacked and defeated Mexican soldiers at San Antonio. Santa Anna sent an army to regain the city. As the army approached, the Texans took refuge in the mission church called the **Alamo**. After 13 days of battle, the Mexicans were victorious and all of the Texans (about 190 men) had been killed.

The Alamo
San Antonio,
Texas

▶ On March 2, 1836, while the battle at the Alamo was raging, Texas leaders declared independence and created the Republic of Texas. Santa Anna signed a treaty recognizing Texas's independence two months later. But the Mexican government said Santa Anna no longer was their leader and refused to recognize the new nation.

▶ The republic was independent until Texas joined the Union in 1845.

American volunteers such as Davy Crockett and Jim Bowie came to aid the Texans and died at the Alamo.

Keywords
- Stephen F. Austin
- Antonio López de Santa Anna
- Alamo

Social Studies

30

LIFE SCIENCE
Human Circulatory System

Blood is a complex fluid. Not only does it carry food and oxygen to each cell, it also removes wastes and fights disease. The **circulatory system** keeps blood flowing and has three main parts:

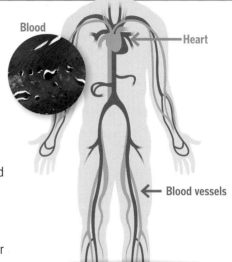

Blood

Heart

Blood vessels

▶ **Blood:** Made from **red blood cells**, which carry oxygen; **white blood cells**, which attack bacteria and other foreign invaders; and **plasma**, which is mostly water. Adults have about eight liters of blood in their bodies.

▶ **Blood Vessels:** These are the "pipes" that carry blood around the body. **Arteries** carry oxygen-rich blood from the heart. **Veins** carry blood from the cells back to the heart, and tiny little vessels called **capillaries** connect the two.

▶ **Heart:** The heart is a muscle about the size of a fist, with four chambers. When the heart beats, blood is pumped through the blood vessels, reaching every part of the body.

Keywords
- circulatory system
- blood
- red blood cells
- white blood cells
- plasma
- blood vessels
- arteries
- veins
- capillaries
- heart

While plants don't have blood, they do have a circulatory system, which carries water and food to the different parts of the plant.

*HELPSTER

The Mexican-American War

In the 19th century, many Americans believed in **Manifest Destiny**, the idea that the United States had the right and duty to expand throughout North America. As Americans pushed west, much of the land they crossed or settled belonged to Mexico. This led to war.

▶ U.S. President James K. Polk asked Congress to declare war on Mexico in 1846 after battles between American and Mexican soldiers in southern Texas.

▶ In 1847, U.S. troops invaded Mexico and fought in Mexico City.

▶ The Treaty of Guadalupe Hidalgo ended the war in 1848. For $15 million, the United States bought the land referred to as the **Mexican Cession**.

▶ In 1853, the United States paid Mexico $10 million for the land called the **Gadsden Purchase**.

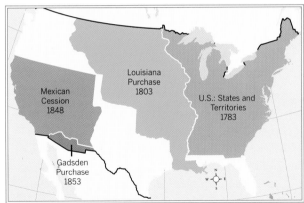

The land that is now California became part of the United States with the Mexican Cession. The discovery of gold in 1848 brought thousands of forty-niners there the next year. In 1850, California had a large enough population from this **gold rush** to apply for statehood.

Keywords
- Manifest Destiny
- Mexican Cession
- Gadsden Purchase
- gold rush

Social Studies

Human Excretory System

The **excretory system** is responsible for getting rid of waste products from the body. It is cleans the blood, removing the leftover salts, gases, and liquids after respiration has taken place in cells.

After food is "burned" by the cells, carbon dioxide, salts, and **urea** are produced. Carbon dioxide is removed by the lungs but the rest of these waste products are taken by the blood to the **kidneys,** which act like filters. Each kidney has more than a million tiny passages called **nephrons,** which screen the blood and remove waste.

Most people have two kidneys, which are bean-shaped organs about the size of your fist. Urea and water is concentrated in the kidneys to form **urine,** which is carried by tubes called **ureters** and stored in the **bladder.** When the bladder is full, the urine passes through the **urethra** and out of the body.

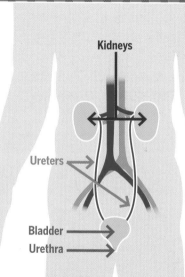

Kidneys

Ureters

Bladder
Urethra

In addition to removing waste, the excretory system helps to keep our bodies cool by making us **perspire** (sweat).

Keywords
- excretory system
- urea
- kidneys
- nephrons
- urine
- ureters
- bladder
- urethra
- perspire

11

Slavery Divides the Nation

Over time, regional differences developed between northern and southern states. Chief among these was the Southern dependence on **slavery** and the Northern rejection of slavery. By the mid-1800s, the North and South were at a breaking point.

Opposition to slavery took several forms, including organized movements, aid to escaping slaves, and active resistance by the enslaved.

FIGHTING SLAVERY

Abolitionists, people who worked to end, or abolish, slavery, started newspapers, made speeches, and wrote books urging the end of slavery. Harriet Beecher Stowe's novel *Uncle Tom's Cabin* was one of the most powerful antislavery works.

The **Underground Railroad** was a network of people and routes to aid escaping slaves. Sympathetic people called conductors, including former slave Harriet Tubman, helped slaves travel from hiding place to hiding place.

Slave revolts, such as the rebellion led by slave Nat Turner in 1831, were a form of violent resistance. In 1859, abolitionist John Brown and followers tried to capture government weapons to give to slaves.

After the Fugitive Slave Act was passed in 1850, escaped slaves were not safe anywhere in the United States. They were forced to go all the way to Canada to find freedom.

Keywords
- slavery
- abolitionists
- *Uncle Tom's Cabin*
- Underground Railroad

Social Studies

32

LIFE SCIENCE
Human Respiratory System

Respiration is the process in which oxygen is used by cells to "burn" food to get energy. Along the way, **carbon dioxide** is released. The **respiratory system** gets **oxygen** from the air to the blood.

In humans, the main organs of the respiratory system are the **lungs**.

Air enters the body through the nose and mouth. At the back of the throat, it passes through a flap called the **epiglottis** and into the **trachea,** or windpipe, which carries it toward the lungs. At the bottom of the trachea, the windpipe splits into two branches called **bronchi.** One is connected to each lung.

Inside the lungs, air moves through smaller and smaller passages, finally reaching tiny air sacs called **alveoli.** Inside these sacs, carbon dioxide, which was removed from the cells of the body by blood, is exchanged for oxygen. The oxygen then gets carried back to the cells by the blood, to be used in respiration. The carbon dioxide is breathed out through the nose and mouth.

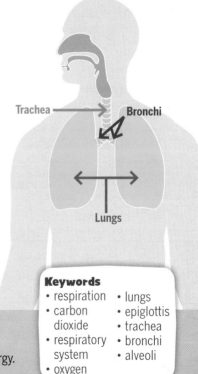

Trachea — Bronchi

Lungs

Keywords
- respiration
- carbon dioxide
- respiratory system
- oxygen
- lungs
- epiglottis
- trachea
- bronchi
- alveoli

Respiration also happens in plants. After they make food by photosynthesis, some of the food is mixed with oxygen to get energy.

The Civil War

Violent disagreements between the North and the South finally led to a civil war—a war between people in the same country. The **Civil War** lasted from 1861 to 1865.

CAUSES

▶ Conflict over slavery, especially whether new states should be slave or free

▶ The southern belief in **states' rights**, that each state—not the federal government—had the right to decide issues such as slavery

▶ Economic differences between the North and South that led to Southern resentment

NORTH

▶ The United States of America, also called the North or the **Union**

▶ President: Abraham Lincoln

▶ Top Generals: George McClellan, Ulysses S. Grant, William Tecumseh Sherman

SOUTH

▶ The Confederate States of America, also called the South or the **Confederacy**

▶ President: Jefferson Davis

▶ Top Generals: Robert E. Lee, Thomas "Stonewall" Jackson, Nathan Bedford Forrest

Keywords
• Civil War
• states' rights
• Union
• Confederacy

Social Studies

33

LIFE SCIENCE
Human Digestive System

Before food can be used by individual animal cells for energy, it must first undergo **digestion.** The **digestive system** has special organs that take complex food molecules and break them down into simpler compounds.

The human digestive system has these main parts:

▶ **Mouth:** Digestion begins as teeth grind the food, mixing it with *saliva*, which has special digestive chemicals.

▶ **Esophagus:** Food travels down a muscular tube from the mouth to the stomach.

▶ **Stomach:** Food is mixed with more digestive juices and acid as it is churned by muscles, breaking it down further.

▶ **Small Intestine:** The partially digested food is mixed with more juices from the **liver** and **pancreas.** By the time it reaches the end, the food has been digested enough for nutrients to be absorbed by the blood.

▶ **Large Intestine:** Undigested food is passed along and water is removed from it. From here, it passes through the **anus** and out of the body.

If you were to stretch out the digestive system of a typical adult, it would be about 30 feet (9 meters) long.

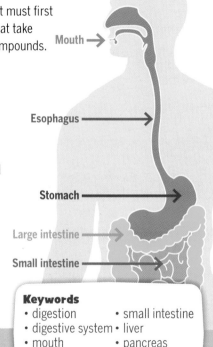

Mouth →

Esophagus →

Stomach →

Large intestine →

Small intestine →

Keywords
- digestion
- digestive system
- mouth
- esophagus
- stomach
- small intestine
- liver
- pancreas
- large intestine
- anus

*HELPSTER

Civil War Time Line

February 1861
Jefferson Davis is named President of the Confederate States of America.

July 1861
First battle—Confederate victory at Bull Run

January 1863
Lincoln issues the **Emancipation Proclamation**, freeing all slaves in the Confederate states.

November 1860
Abraham Lincoln is elected President of the United States of America.

September 1864
Union captures Atlanta; Sherman's March to the Sea.

1860   1861   1862   1863   1864   1865

December 1860
South Carolina is the first state to **secede**.

April 1861
The Confederate attack on Fort Sumter begins the war.

1862
Union victories at Shiloh and Antietam

July 1863
Union victory at Gettysburg marks turning point of the war.

April 1865
War ends when Lee surrenders to Grant at Appomattox Court House, Virginia.

March 1861
Lincoln's inauguration. Seven states seceded before he was sworn in as president.

1862–1863
Confederate victories at Fredericksburg and Chancellorsville

Social Studies

More Americans lost their lives in the Civil War than in any other American war. More than 360,000 Union and 250,000 Confederate soldiers died.

Keywords
- secede
- Emancipation Proclamation

✴HELPSTER

34

LIFE SCIENCE
Photosynthesis

Photosynthesis is the process that green plants and certain bacteria use to make food using energy from the sun. These living things are called **producers** because they make the food that animals need to eat.

In green plants, photosynthesis happens in a part of the cell called the **chloroplast.** Here a green substance called **chlorophyll** takes in energy from the sun and uses it to combine water and **carbon dioxide** from the air to make a simple sugar. During photosynthesis, **oxygen** is released from the plant. The sugar stores the sun's energy as food for the plant to use at a later time. When people and animals eat plants, they use the stored energy as fuel.

Step 1: Plants take in water through their roots. It flows through the plant to the leaves.

Step 2: Plants take in carbon dioxide through their leaves, and it goes into the cells, mixing with water.

Step 3: Sunlight is absorbed by the cells' chloroplasts. Energy from it is used to combine the water and carbon dioxide to make sugar and oxygen.

Step 4: Sugar is stored in the plant, and oxygen is released into the air.

The word *photosynthesis* comes from two Greek words. *Photo* means "light" and *synthesis* means "putting together." The whole word means "putting together using light."

Keywords
- photosynthesis
- producers
- chloroplast
- chlorophyll
- carbon dioxide
- oxygen

✳️**HELPSTER**

Abraham Lincoln

Abraham Lincoln, the 16th president of the United States, led the nation through the Civil War. Many historians rate him as the greatest U. S. president.

8. Assassinated on April 14, 1865

1. Born in Kentucky on February 12, 1809

7. Most famous speech: **Gettysburg Address**, November 19, 1863

2. Grew up in frontier Indiana

6. Signed the **Emancipation Proclamation** on January 1, 1863, freeing all slaves in Confederate states

3. Practiced law in Illinois

5. Elected President of the United States in 1860, leading to the secession of seven states

4. Came to national attention when he debated Stephen A. Douglas in the 1858 Senate race

Social Studies

President Lincoln was shot by actor John Wilkes Booth 41 days after his second inauguration.

Keywords
- Abraham Lincoln
- Emancipation Proclamation
- Gettysburg Address

HELPSTER

LIFE SCIENCE
Basic Needs

All living things, whether they are plants or animals, have certain basic needs that they must get from their **environment** in order to live. If any of these are missing, they will not survive for long.

All green plants get their **energy** from the sun. Using the sunlight, plant cells make their own food. They convert water and two gases from the air (**carbon dioxide** and **oxygen**) into simple sugars. Most plants also need certain **nutrients** from the soil to grow mature and healthy.

Animals do not make their own food. They get their energy and nutrients from eating plants or other animals. In addition, all animals need water to drink and oxygen from the air to breathe. Many animals also need some type of shelter to protect them from the environment, although some carry their own shelter with them.

All living things also require a certain amount of space to grow and move in. If they are too crowded, they must seek a new environment, if they can, to survive.

Keywords
- environment
- energy
- carbon dioxide
- oxygen
- nutrients

✳**HELPSTER**

Reconstruction

Following the Civil War, the nation—led by former vice president Andrew Johnson—had to put itself back together again. This period, called **Reconstruction**, lasted from 1865 to 1877.

▶ The 4 million people formerly enslaved now faced numerous problems. Many worked for white farmers as sharecroppers.

▶ The **Freedmen's Bureau** helped former slaves "get on their feet."

▶ Southern laws called **black codes** limited the rights of former slaves. Groups such as the **Ku Klux Klan** terrorized African-Americans.

▶ The nation passed three constitutional amendments: The **13th Amendment** abolished slavery. The **14th** gave citizenship to everyone born in the United States, including former slaves. The **15th** said no one could be denied the right to vote because of race.

▶ Union troops stayed in the South until 1877. When they left, segregation separated African-Americans from whites in much of southern life.

A primary school for freed slaves

The Granger Collection, New York

Carpetbaggers were Northerners who went to the South during Reconstruction. Scalawags were white Southerners who supported Reconstruction. Although members of both groups sincerely wanted to help, others sought to profit from the situation, and both terms have a negative connotation.

Keywords
• Reconstruction
• Freedmen's Bureau
• black codes
• Ku Klux Klan
• 13th, 14th, 15th Amendments

Social Studies

LIFE SCIENCE
Cells

All living things are made up of tiny building blocks called **cells.** Some living things, like bacteria, are made of only one cell. Humans on the other hand are made up of trillions of cells.

While plant and animal cells have some important differences, they both have the following structures in them.

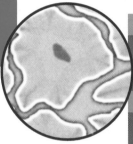

Plant cell

Cell Membrane	The outer protective layer of the cell.
Cytoplasm	A thin gel made mostly of water with chemicals dissolved in it. It transports material around the cell.
Mitochondria	Makes the energy to power the cell.
Vacuole	A place for storing food and other material in a cell.
Nucleus	Controls most cell functions. It also contains DNA, the material that determines what an organism will look like.

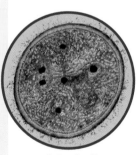

Animal cell

Plant cells also contain **chloroplasts**, which convert sunlight to food, and have a thick cell wall surrounding the membrane.

Keywords
- cells
- cell membrane
- cytoplasm
- mitochondria
- vacuole
- nucleus
- chloroplasts

✳ **HELPSTER**

Industrialization

The **Industrial Revolution** started to change American life around 1800. Throughout the 19th century, the nation became more and more industrialized.

▶ In 1790, Englishman Samuel Slater built America's first factory, a textile mill, in Rhode Island. The factory system soon changed how Americans worked.

▶ Inventor Eli Whitney developed **mass production** by designing products with interchangeable parts. Workers controlled machines that produced the same part over and over again. This allowed products to be made faster than ever before.

▶ Inventions and innovations in transportation included canals and steam railroads. By 1869, the coasts were linked by a **transcontinental railroad**.

▶ Steel replaced iron to build railroad tracks, and Andrew Carnegie built a giant steel industry in Pittsburgh, Pennsylvania, in the mid-1800s. At the same time, John D. Rockefeller consolidated the oil business into a giant monopoly.

▶ Industrial cities grew near needed resources such as iron ore and coal.

The Granger Collection, New York

Calico printing in a cotton mill, 1834

Industry changed business: Companies needed money to expand, so they formed corporations and sold shares, or stock, to investors.

Keywords
• Industrial Revolution
• mass production
• transcontinental railroad

Social Studies

LIFE SCIENCE
Life in the Past

Fossils are the remains of living things that have become preserved in stone. They are "windows into the past," giving scientists clues about how life and the environment have changed over time.

Most fossils are those of animals and plants that are **extinct.** When something is extinct, all of the individuals that make up its **species** are dead. By comparing the fossils found in rocks with animals and plants that are alive today, scientists can figure out how extinct animals moved, grew, ate, and even reproduced.

Fossils can also give scientists clues on how the environment and climate on Earth have changed over time. Fossils of seashells high on a hill tell that there was once an ocean there, and fossilized plants can tell if an area was a desert or swamp.

Keywords
- fossils
- extinct
- species

Immigration

From the mid-1800s to the early 1900s, more than 20 million immigrants arrived in the United States. Worried about **immigration**, the government passed laws regulating the number of immigrants allowed to come in from specific countries.

▶ Europeans made up the vast majority of these immigrants. At first, they came from northern and western Europe (Great Britain and Scandinavia), later from southern, central, and eastern Europe. Most came through New York's **Ellis Island** and lived in the growing industrial cities.

▶ Beginning with the gold rush, Chinese immigrants came to California to work. Starting in 1863, the Central Pacific Railroad hired more than 25,000 Chinese immigrants to help build the **transcontinental railroad**. By the late 1800s, laws prevented, then limited Asian immigration.

▶ Smaller numbers of immigrants came from Mexico and Central and South America to find work. Most settled in the Southwest and West.

Ellis Island immigration station

Social Studies

Urban areas also changed because of a great migration of African-Americans from the South to northern and midwestern cities in the early 1900s.

Keywords
• immigration
• Ellis Island
• transcontinental railroad

LIFE SCIENCE
Life Cycles

Every living thing has its own **life cycle** or pattern of growth, which includes a number of different **stages.** The life cycle of a typical flowering plant includes the following stages:

1. **Seed Germination:** When water and temperature conditions are right, a seed buried in the soil will begin to grow, producing a new plant.

2. **Growth:** Using sunlight, water, carbon dioxide from the air, and minerals from the soil, plants grow and mature.

3. **Flower Formation:** Eventually, a flower forms, which has male pollen and female egg cells in it.

4. **Seed Production:** When the pollen from one flower reaches the egg of another, fertilization takes place. Changes happen inside the flower and new seeds form, starting the cycle again.

An insect life cycle begins when an adult lays eggs. They hatch, go through **metamorphosis,** and then become new adults.

Keywords
- life cycle
- stages
- metamorphosis

The Labor Movement

As more people worked in industry rather than for themselves, new problems emerged. Workers and business owners reacted to the problems, sometimes constructively but sometimes not.

THE PROBLEMS

▶ Factory employees worked long hours for low wages.

▶ Almost 20 percent of factory workers were children (who worked instead of going to school).

▶ Working conditions were often unsafe.

▶ Because there were many people looking for jobs, factory owners could fire those who complained and hire new workers.

THE REACTIONS

▶ Some workers went on **strike** to protest unfair or unsafe conditions.

▶ Workers joined together in **labor unions** to gain strength in numbers. In the 1880s, under the leadership of **Samuel Gompers**, unions of skilled laborers joined together in a federation.

▶ Some strikes led to violence between union workers and industry owners.

▶ Until the reforms of the early 1900s, the government sided with industry.

Social Studies

In 1886, Gompers's federation of unions became the American Federation of Labor (AFL).

Keywords
• strike
• labor unions
• Samuel Gompers

✳HELPSTER

Classification

Scientists set up systems of **classification** to help them organize groups of living things. One way of classifying animals is to separate them based on the type of food they eat.

Carnivores are animals that eat only meat. They are usually **predators** that have special adaptations to help them hunt, like sharp claws or teeth. Hawks, sharks, lions, snakes, and polar bears are all carnivores.

Herbivores are animals that eat only plants. They have special adaptations like flat teeth or strong jaws for grinding leaves and seeds. Cows, horses, sheep, and many insects are herbivores.

Omnivores are animals that eat both meat and plants. Their bodies have adaptations that allow them to eat both types of food. Some typical omnivores include many turtles, chimpanzees, pigs, and humans.

Keywords
- classification
- carnivores
- predators
- herbivores
- omnivores

Animals can also be classified in other ways, such as the way they move or the type of covering they have on their bodies.

World War I

In 1914, war began in southern Europe and spread across the continent. Before the war's end in 1918, the United States had entered the conflict, which would be known as the Great War or **World War I**.

▶ For protection, European countries had joined together in alliances: the **Allied Powers** (chiefly Britain, France, Belgium, Serbia, and Russia) and the **Central Powers** (Austria-Hungary, Germany, and Turkey).

▶ When Austria-Hungary declared war on Serbia, their allies joined the conflict.

Trench warfare in World War I

▶ At first, the United States tried to stay out of the war. When German ships attacked American ships, the United States entered the war on the side of the Allied Powers. Eventually, more than 100 countries were part of the conflict.

▶ Germany surrendered and war ended on November 11, 1918.

▶ The **Treaty of Versailles**, which ended the war, established an international forum called the **League of Nations**. Many Americans opposed the League of Nations, so the United States did not join.

In this deadly war, 65 million soldiers were involved, 8.6 million were killed, and 20 million were wounded. France, Germany, Russia, and Austria-Hungary each lost more than one million lives, while more than 116,000 American lives were lost.

Social Studies

Keywords
- World War I
- Allied Powers
- Central Powers
- Treaty of Versailles
- League of Nations

40

LIFE SCIENCE
Adaptations

Animals and plants have special adaptations that help them survive in the environments in which they live. These can be either **physical adaptations** or **behavioral adaptations**.

Physical adaptations are usually special body parts or structures that help an animal or plant survive.

A shark has a streamlined body shape and razor-sharp teeth to help it swim fast and hunt its prey.

A polar bear has thick white fur to protect it from the cold and help it blend in with the snow.

A cactus has a thick stem with sharp needles on it. The stem has special cells that store water so that the cactus can survive in the dry desert, and the needles keep the plant from being eaten.

Behavioral adaptations are the way plants and animals act to help them survive.

Alaskan seagulls **migrate** to warmer climates when winter comes.

Opossums play dead—play possum—by going into a comalike state to avoid attacks. Many predators do not eat dead animals.

Desert lilies go dormant to escape drought.

Adaptations do not happen quickly. They often take thousands of years to develop as small changes are inherited by one generation of living things from the previous one.

Keywords
- physical adaptations
- behavioral adaptations
- migrate

✳HELPSTER

The Great Depression

The years after World War I were a prosperous time in the United States. Beginning in 1929, however, the nation entered a major economic depression. There was high unemployment, low economic growth, and little money in circulation.

- On October 29, 1929, the stock market crashed. Investors lost millions of dollars and businesses failed.

- Many banks closed down, and people lost all of their savings.

- Like a spiral, failing businesses led to more **unemployment**. When people lost their jobs, they could not pay their bills. That caused more businesses to fail.

- Elected in 1932, President Franklin D. Roosevelt proposed the **New Deal**. Congress passed laws to create government programs to give people jobs and financial support.

- The New Deal turned the economy around and ended the **Great Depression** by 1941.

U.S. Unemployment 1929–1945

Number of People (millions) vs. Year (1929, 1931, 1933, 1935, 1937, 1939, 1941, 1943, 1945)

Keywords
- unemployment
- New Deal
- Great Depression

Social Studies

41

LIFE SCIENCE
Ecosystems

An **ecosystem** is an interconnected web made up of all the living and nonliving things found in an environment. A change in one part of an ecosystem will affect all the other parts.

An ecosystem has a **community** made up of different **populations** of plants and animals that live together and affect each other in different ways. In some cases, they support each other. (For example: Cows eat grass.) In other cases, they compete with each other for food and other **resources.** (For example: Birds and mice both eat the same seeds.)

One of the most important relationships in an ecosystem is between animals that are **predator** and **prey.** A predator is an animal that eats another animal. Prey is the animal that is eaten.

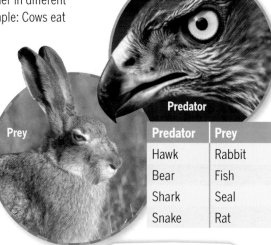

Predator

Prey

Predator	Prey
Hawk	Rabbit
Bear	Fish
Shark	Seal
Snake	Rat

Within a healthy ecosystem, there is a balance between the number of animals that are predators and those that are prey.

Keywords
- ecosystem
- community
- populations
- resources
- predator
- prey

✳HELPSTER

1

World War II

World War II broke out in Europe in 1939 and by 1940 had spread to the Pacific. In 1941, the United States entered the war and fought in both Europe and the Pacific until 1945.

▶ In the 1930s, dictators who ruled Germany (Hitler), the Soviet Union (Stalin), Italy (Mussolini), and Japan (Hirohito) began invading other countries.

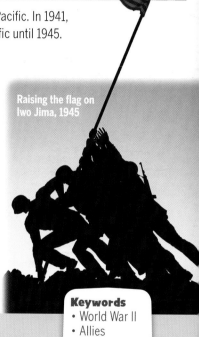

Raising the flag on Iwo Jima, 1945

▶ Britain and France declared war on Germany after the invasion of Poland in 1939. The United States entered the war when Japan attacked Pearl Harbor in 1941.

▶ At war were the **Allies** (Britain, France, the United States, the Soviet Union, and many others) and the **Axis Powers** (led by Germany, Italy, and Japan).

▶ The Allies won the war in Europe in 1945 after a push that began on D-day—June 6, 1944—when Allied forces landed in France. Allied victory came in the Pacific later in 1945 after the United States dropped two **atomic bombs** on Japan.

Hitler's Nazi Party attempted to exterminate the Jewish people and others whom they blamed for Germany's problems. They killed 12 million people, 6 million of them Jews, in what is called the **Holocaust**.

Keywords
- World War II
- Allies
- Axis Powers
- atomic bomb
- Holocaust

Social Studies

✳HELPSTER

The Cold War

Following World War II, another war pitted the United States and its allies in the free world against the Soviet Union and the **Communist** world. This was the **Cold War**, a political and economic battle between two superpowers and their allies.

The Berlin Wall

▶ After the war, the Soviet Union cut off the countries of Eastern Europe so that people said they were "behind an iron curtain." Germany was divided into two nations, one free (West Germany) and one Communist (East Germany). In 1961, a concrete wall—the **Berlin Wall**—was built between them.

▶ The superpowers competed in an arms race for military power. In the 1962 **Cuban Missile Crisis**, U.S. president John F. Kennedy blockaded Cuba, the Soviet Union's ally, until the Soviets agreed to remove missiles it had placed there.

▶ In the 1970s and 1980s, world leaders worked to end the Cold War. The Berlin Wall came down in 1989 and Germany was reunited. Eastern European countries gained new freedoms. And in 1991, the Soviet Union broke up into separate nations.

The United States fought two "hot" wars against Communism during the Cold War era: the Korean War (1950–1953) and the Vietnam War (1964–1973). In the Korean War, free-world forces kept the independence of South Korea. In the Vietnam War, Communist North Vietnam succeeded in taking over South Korea.

Keywords
- Communist
- Cold War
- Berlin Wall
- Cuban Missile Crisis

Social Studies

43

Science **Keywords** (continued)

Civil Rights

The Granger Collection, New York

Beginning in the 1950s, many Americans organized to gain their **civil rights**, the rights all Americans are guaranteed by the Constitution.

▶ The 1954 Supreme Court decision ***Brown v. Board of Education*** ended the segregation that had kept African-American children in separate schools from white children.

▶ The 1955 bus boycott in Birmingham, Alabama, led by civil rights leader **Dr. Martin Luther King Jr.**, was part of a long but successful struggle to end segregation in public places.

▶ Across the South, King led nonviolent marches and other protests for integration and voting rights.

▶ Others who demanded equal rights included American Indians and the farmworkers led by **César Chávez**. Women's rights groups worked for equal opportunities for women on the job and in other areas. Americans with disabilities and gay Americans challenged the discrimination they faced in their daily lives.

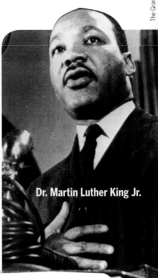

Dr. Martin Luther King Jr.

The 1964 Civil Rights Act led to important changes in American life by making it illegal to segregate public places or deny jobs to people because of race. The 1965 Voting Rights Act made discrimination in voting illegal.

Social Studies

Keywords
• civil rights
• *Brown v. Board of Education*
• Martin Luther King Jr.
• César Chávez

Science Keywords

air pressure	19	carbon cycle	20

air pressure 19
alloys 34
alveoli 10
amplitude 45
anus 9
artery 12
asexual reproduction 13
asteroids 28
atmosphere 19
atomic number 32
atom 31, 32
attract 44
bacteria 21
barometer 19
behavioral adaptation 2
bladder 11
blood 12
blood vessels 12
bronchi 10
capillary 12
carbohydrate 14

carbon cycle 20
carbon dioxide 7, 8, 10, 20, 36
carnivore 3
community 1
cell 6
cell membrane 6
chemical changes 36
chemical formula 33
chlorophyll 8
chloroplast 6, 8
chromosphere 26
circuit 37, 43
circulatory system 12
classification 3
clay 24
closed system 37
cloud cover 18
comet 28
compound 33
condensation 16

condense 35
conductivity 34
conductor 43
constellations 29
convection cycle 17
corona 26
crust 22
crystal 23
cytoplasm 6
decomposer 24
density 31
diabetes 15
digestion 9, 36
digestive system 9
disease 15
drag 38
ecosystem 1, 37
effort 40
egg 13
electricity 43
electromagnet 44

element 32, 33
ellipses 28
embryo 13
energy 7
environment 7
epiglottis 10
esophagus 9
evaporation 16
excretory system 11
extinct 5
fat 14
fermentation 36
fertilize 13
force 38, 39
fossil 5
fossil fuel 20
frequency 45
freshwater 16
friction 38
front 18
fulcrum 40

Globalization

Today, people, ideas, money, and products move around the globe more quickly and thoroughly than ever before. Thinking globally instead of nationally means that people's lives are intertwined internationally—for better or for worse.

TRADE
▶ Nations have signed free trade agreements such as NAFTA (North American Free Trade Agreement).

▶ Nations join together in trade organizations such as OPEC (Organization of Petroleum Exporting Countries) and the WTO (World Trade Organization).

RESOURCES
▶ Developed nations such as the United States and rapidly expanding nations such as China seek the resources they need—petroleum, for example—outside of their own borders.

POLITICS
▶ Some nations have formed political alliances such as the European Union.

▶ **Terrorism** has become an enemy without national borders.

BUSINESS
▶ Multinational corporations operate across national boundaries.

▶ Businesses outsource work to lower-paid workers in other countries.

The **Internet** is part of what makes globalization possible. This global computer network came into being in the 1960s, spread rapidly after the development of e-mail in 1972 and the TCP/IP networking protocol in the 1970s, and was widespread by the 1990s.

Social Studies

Keywords
• globalization
• terrorism
• Internet

Science Contents (continued)

Notes

Science Contents

Math Contents

Taking Notes

As you do research, it's important to **take notes** on what you find. Well-organized, useful notes make writing a paper easier. Here are some tips on taking good notes.

▶ Use a fresh notebook page, sheet of paper, or note card for each new source. At the top of the card, write the subject of the information and the name of the source.

▶ Do not copy exact sentences from your sources. That makes it less likely that you will accidentally plagiarize someone else's work.

▶ If possible, read the source once straight through without taking notes. Then go back and take notes on the second reading.

▶ If you're using sources that you own, circle, highlight, or underline information that you think is really important. That makes it easy to find later.

▶ Write down ideas that come to you while you're taking notes. You may not remember them later.

You might want to use a **learning log** like this to take your notes.

Learning Log

Notes	Thoughts
Put facts, quotes, or information from a source here.	Put any questions, ideas, analysis, or responses you have here.

Reliable Web sites include government, nationally known organization, museum, and university. Neither blogs nor Web sites maintained by small, unknown groups are considered reliable.

Keywords
• take notes
• learning log

Math Contents (continued)

Watching TV

Playing soccer

Playing videogames

Reading

RESEARCH
Primary and Secondary Sources

Sources are the books, articles, Web sites, and other things you research to write a report (or, less often, to write a story or an essay). There are two main kinds of sources: **primary sources** and **secondary sources**. Reference materials are always secondary sources. The chart below tells you about each kind and gives some examples.

Kind of Source	What It Is	Examples
Primary source	a firsthand account of an event or a life	letters, diaries, memoirs, journals, interviews, autobiographies, news reports from the time the event took place, poems, songs, artwork, photographs, artifacts
Secondary source	a secondhand account of an event or a life (Usually, secondary sources are based on primary sources.)	biographies, articles, and books about an event; recent news reports that recount an event that took place in the past

Imagine that you are writing a report on the Westminster Kennel Club Dog Show in New York City. What are some sources you could use?

A good research report usually includes both primary and secondary sources. However, if it is difficult to find primary sources about your topic, it's okay to use only secondary sources.

Keywords
- primary sources
- secondary sources

Math Keywords

RESEARCH
Reference Books and More

Most research starts with **reference books** and other reference materials.
Here is a list of common materials and how to use them.

Reference Material	What It Is
Encyclopedia	One book or a series of books containing facts about many topics. Each topic is called an encyclopedia entry. Entries are organized alphabetically. Use an encyclopedia to do the initial research on a topic.
Atlas	A book of maps. Use atlases to look up a country, state, or other place, or to find landforms and bodies of water. Some atlases contain information about weather. Historical atlases contain information about historical places.
Almanac	A collections of facts, usually about a single country or a certain year. Use almanacs to get up-to-date facts about a place or time.
CD-ROM	Reference materials that are stored on a CD. Often, the information is more up-to-date than that in books. Use recent CD-ROMs to find the most up-to-date encyclopedia entries, maps, and almanac entries.

All these reference materials can be found in a library. Versions of them also can be found online. Be sure to use only reliable Web sites as online reference sources.

Keywords
- reference book
- encyclopedia
- atlas
- almanac
- CD-ROM

HELPSTER

Math **Keywords** (continued)

PUBLIC SPEAKING
Speech Structure

Preparing for **public speaking** is a lot like preparing for writing. It includes many of the same steps.

▶ Decide what you want to speak about. If necessary, research your topic. Take notes. Use more than one source of information. Make sure your speech has a central focus.

▶ Organize your important ideas and evidence. Come up with a thesis or main idea. Create a detailed outline.

▶ Use the same **structure** for public speaking that you would use for a written essay. Have an introductory section, a supporting section, and a concluding section. But don't just write an essay and read it. Public speaking is about speaking, not reading.

▶ Carefully consider your **point of view**. In a speech, listeners assume that the viewpoints you mention are your own. Make clear the differences between your own opinions and those of others.

Thesis: Dogs can inspire people.

Intro: Talk about how pets have inspired people to do great things.

Support: Two examples and my own experience.

Conclusion: The bond between a dog and a person can be so strong that it changes the person's life.

A speech should be leaner and meaner than a written essay. Don't overload it with details. That just confuses and bores your audience. On the other hand, don't skimp on details. Use enough to give your speech some depth.

Keywords
• public speaking
• structure
• point of view

*HELPSTER

Place Value

Place value tells you how much each digit in a number is worth.
A **period** is a three-digit grouping.

You can use the period names to help you read and write the
word name for the distance.

Sun

Billions Period			Millions Period			Thousands Period			Ones Period		
Hundreds	Tens	Ones	Hundreds	Tens	Ones	Hundreds	Tens	Ones	Hundreds	Tens	Ones
			5	7	9	0	9	1	7	5	

↑ ↑
Commas are used to separate the periods.

The distance from
the sun to Mercury is
57,909,175 kilometers.

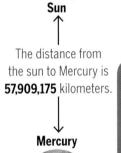

Mercury

READ "Fifty-seven million, nine hundred nine thousand, one hundred seventy-five kilometers."
▶ The 5 is in the ten millions place.
▶ Its value is 5×10 million, or 50,000,000.

Think of the first comma from the right as the thousand comma and say
"thousand" when you see it. The next comma, moving left, is the million
comma. Say "million" when you see it. The billion comma comes next.

Keywords
• place value
• period
• commas

Math

PUBLIC SPEAKING
Adjusting Your Style

You can adjust your **speaking style** to suit any purpose, audience, or occasion. Consider all these parts of your speaking style.

▶ **Rate:** Speak more slowly for larger, more formal occasions. Speak a little faster when you want to persuade.

▶ **Volume:** Speak loudly before a large audience. Speak more softly before a small group.

▶ **Vocabulary:** Use a formal vocabulary for a formal occasion. In a very informal setting, you can use a little slang.

▶ **Diction:** For a formal occasion, make sure your grammar is perfect. Use everyday speech for an informal occasion.

▶ **Pitch:** The tone of your speaking voice should be pleasant. Try not to make it too high or too low.

▶ **Gestures:** Use hand and arm gestures to help convey information. Don't get carried away, though. You don't want people to be so busy watching your gestures that they don't listen to your words.

When you have an assembly at school or watch a speech on TV, pay attention to the speaker's style. Think about the six points above. Overall, what grade (from A to F) would you give the speaker?

Keywords
- speaking style
- rate
- volume
- vocabulary
- diction
- pitch
- gestures

✳️HELPSTER

Comparing and Ordering

You can use **place value** to compare and order numbers.

The scores for three figure skaters are 80.5 points, 83.3 points, and 83.24 points. Which score is least in value?

Align the numbers by place value.

▶ Begin at the left.

▶ Find the place where the digits are different.

▶ Compare these digits.

same

8	0	.	5	
8	3	.	3	
8	3	.	2	4

2 < 3, so 83.24 < 83.3.

0 < 3, so 80.5 is the least in value.

The numbers arranged in order from **least value** to **greatest value**:

   80.5   83.24   83.3.

The numbers arranged in order from **greatest** to **least**:

   83.3   83.24   80.5.

On a **number line**, numbers are arranged in order from least to greatest value, moving from left to right.

7.0 7.1 7.2 7.3 7.4 7.5 7.6 7.7 7.8 7.9 8.0

7.1 < 7.5 and 7.5 < 7.9

Keywords
- place value
- least value
- greatest value
- number line

Math

✳HELPSTER

2

Speaking Style

When it comes to **public speaking**, style counts for a lot. Different styles work for different situations. Consider these three things as you prepare for public speaking.

▶ **Your Purpose:** Do you need to inform, persuade, or entertain your audience? Each purpose requires a slightly different style. Informative speaking tends to be serious. Persuasive speaking tends to be compelling. Entertaining speaking tends to be informal and amusing.

▶ **Your Audience:** To whom will you be speaking? You might adopt a different tone for, say, the Parent Teacher Association than you would for your classmates. It's always important to keep your audience in mind you're when preparing.

▶ **Your Occasion:** Formal occasions, such as performances or graduations, require more formal speaking. Informal occasions (for instance, classroom discussions) require less preparation.

For hints on how to adjust your **speaking style**, see the next page.

Keep these two important points in mind when you speak in public. First, speak clearly. The most important thing is that people understand what you say. Second, make eye contact with your audience. Try to look at them instead of at the ground or the ceiling. (If that makes you too nervous and it's a large audience, look just above their heads.)

Keywords
• public speaking
• audience
• speaking style

✳HELPSTER

Fractions

A **fraction** is a number that represents part of a whole or part of a group.
The **denominator** is the bottom number. It's the total number of equal parts in the whole.
The **numerator** is the top number and tells how many parts are being discussed.

In the pizza pie,
5 of the 8 slices remain.

$\frac{5}{8}$ ← slices of pizza pie that remain
  ← total number of equal slices

So $\frac{5}{8}$ of the pizza pie remains.

In the bowl of fruit,
4 of the 9 pieces of fruit are apples.

$\frac{4}{9}$ ← number of apples
  ← total pieces of fruit

So $\frac{4}{9}$ of the pieces of fruit are apples.

You can represent a fraction with a point on a number line.

Notice that the distance between 0 and 1 has been divided into 6 equal parts. Point A is 5 parts away from 0. So point A represents $\frac{5}{6}$.

Keywords
• fraction
• denominator
• numerator

3

WRITING
Answering Document-Based Questions

Document-based questions appear on standardized tests. These questions present a variety of documents, such as maps, charts, and historical texts, about a particular topic. First you answer short questions about the information contained in each document. Usually, you then use information from all the documents to write an essay.

Being able to answer document-based questions well is a **test-taking skill**.
Here are some tips to help you.

▶ First consider the topic. What do you already know about the topic?
  Keep your prior knowledge in mind as you read.

▶ Read each document carefully. If the document is a map, chart, or graph,
  make sure you understand the information it presents.

▶ Underline any important facts, details, or ideas you find in a document.

▶ For the essay, use what you already know and the information in the documents to create a clear
  thesis statement. Don't start writing until you have thought through and decided on your thesis.

▶ Before writing, create a brief outline for your essay. List all the information you want to use from the
  documents. The outline will help you stay on track as you write.

Reading comprehension is particularly important for
document-based questions. If you don't understand one of
the documents you're given, use reading strategies, including
rereading and finding the main idea, to help you.

Keywords
- document-based questions
- test-taking skill
- reading comprehension

Equivalent Fractions

Equivalent fractions are fractions that name the same amount. These fraction strips show that $\frac{1}{2}$, $\frac{2}{4}$, and $\frac{4}{8}$ are equivalent fractions.

To find equivalent fractions, multiply or divide the numerator and denominator by the same non-zero number (a **common factor**).

To write a fraction in lowest terms, divide the numerator and denominator by their **greatest common factor**.

Finding Equivalent Fractions by Multiplying	Finding Equivalent Fractions by Dividing
$\frac{1}{3} = \frac{1 \times 2}{3 \times 2} = \frac{2}{6}$ $\qquad$ $\frac{3}{4} = \frac{3 \times 3}{4 \times 3} = \frac{9}{12}$	$\frac{6}{18} = \frac{6 \div 6}{18 \div 6} = \frac{1}{3}$ $\qquad$ $\frac{20}{25} = \frac{20 \div 5}{25 \div 5} = \frac{4}{5}$

To compare two fractions, cross multiply. Multiply the numerator of each fraction by the denominator of the other one. Write the products above each numerator. The higher product is above the larger fraction. If the products are the same, the fractions are equivalent. Compare $\frac{2}{3}$ and $\frac{5}{6}$: $15 > 12$, so $\frac{5}{6} > \frac{2}{3}$.

Keywords
- equivalent fractions
- common factor
- greatest common factor

Math

4

WRITING
Formal Letters

Write **formal**, or **business**, **letters** to companies or groups, or to adults who are not personally known to you. Also use them for adults with whom you are on formal terms, such as your principal. Every formal letter follows the format shown here.

Jacob Smith
4 River Road
Canine, CA 93684
October 5, 2006

Always put your name, address, and the date at the top.

Director
Lost Dog Foundation
26 Doghouse Lane
Canine, CA 93681

Below your name and address, put the name and address of the person to whom you are writing.

Dear Director:

If you know a person's last name, use it (as in Dear Ms. Lang) in the greeting, or salutation. If you know only a person's title, such as director, use that. If you know nothing about the person you are writing to, use "To Whom It May Concern." Always end the greeting with a colon.

I am writing concerning my lost dog, Sam. I understand that your foundation will organize a search-and-reward effort for lost dogs. I would like to request such an effort for Sam. He has been missing for a week and I would really like to find him. I can't organize a large search party on my own. Nor can I afford to pay a large reward. I have put up flyers in the neighborhood, but they have not gotten results.

Formal letters should be short and to the point. Give as much information about yourself or your situation as possible. Then be clear about what you want. Always end with a thank-you.

Please let me know if you would be willing to take on my case. I would do anything to find Sam. I would be happy to help the effort in any way I could. Thank you very much.

Sincerely,
Jacob Smith

If your letter is typed, also type your name. But leave a space above to sign it by hand.

Always close with "Sincerely," "Yours truly," or "Very truly yours." Capitalize only the first word in a closing.

Keywords
• formal letter
• business letter

53

NUMBER SENSE AND OPERATIONS
Multiplying Fractions

When you **multiply** two **fractions** that are less than one, the product is always less than either fraction.

James planted vegetables in $\frac{1}{2}$ of his garden. He planted tomatoes in $\frac{3}{5}$ of the area where he planted his vegetables. What fraction of James's entire garden did he plant with tomatoes?

The answer is $\frac{3}{5}$ of $\frac{1}{2}$ of the total garden, or $\frac{3}{5} \times \frac{1}{2}$.

First multiply the numerators. Then multiply the denominators.

$$\frac{1}{2} \times \frac{3}{5} = \frac{1 \times 3}{2 \times 5} = \frac{3}{10}$$

James planted $\frac{3}{10}$ of his garden with tomatoes.

Vegetables

Tomatoes

The word *of* usually tells you to multiply.
Whole numbers can be numerators with 1 as their denominator.
You can think of a fraction as a division problem. The numerator is the dividend. The denominator is the divisor.

If there are 28 children in a class and $\frac{1}{4}$ of them wear red shirts, how many kids are wearing red shirts?

$\frac{1}{4}$ of $28 = \frac{1}{4} \times \frac{28}{1} = \frac{28}{4} = 28 \div 4 = 7$ kids are wearing red shirts.

Keywords
• multiply fractions

Math

*HELPSTER

5

Research Essays

Research essays are essays based on research that you have done about a topic. Follow these steps.

▶ Find and use at least three good **sources** of information. These could include books, magazine articles, newspaper articles, encyclopedia entries, and reliable Web sites.

▶ Take notes on your research. See page 60 for more information.

▶ Include a **bibliography**, a list of your sources. Here's how to format the sources.

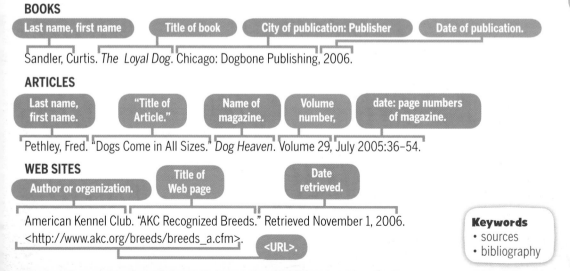

BOOKS

| Last name, first name | Title of book | City of publication: Publisher | Date of publication. |

Sandler, Curtis. *The Loyal Dog*. Chicago: Dogbone Publishing, 2006.

ARTICLES

| Last name, first name. | "Title of Article." | Name of magazine. | Volume number, | date: page numbers of magazine. |

Pethley, Fred. "Dogs Come in All Sizes." *Dog Heaven*. Volume 29, July 2005:36–54.

WEB SITES

| Author or organization. | Title of Web page | Date retrieved. |

American Kennel Club. "AKC Recognized Breeds." Retrieved November 1, 2006. <http://www.akc.org/breeds/breeds_a.cfm>. <URL>.

Keywords
• sources
• bibliography

Dividing Fractions

When you divide two fractions that are less than one, remember:

▶ If the divisor is less than the **dividend**, the **quotient** will be greater than one.

▶ If the divisor is greater than the dividend, the quotient will be less than one.

The model shows how to divide $\frac{2}{3}$ by $\frac{1}{6}$. ⟶

> The rectangle is divided into thirds and sixths. Notice that $\frac{2}{3}$ of the rectangle has been shaded blue. Count the number of $\frac{1}{6}$'s in $\frac{2}{3}$.
>
> There are four $\frac{1}{6}$'s in $\frac{2}{3}$. So, $\frac{2}{3} \div \frac{1}{6} = 4$. ($\frac{1}{6}$ fits into $\frac{2}{3}$ four times.)

Two numbers that have a product of 1 are **reciprocals**. $\frac{5}{9}$ and $\frac{9}{5}$ are reciprocals since $\frac{5}{9} \times \frac{9}{5} = 1$. You can use reciprocals with multiplication to divide fractions.

reciprocal ⟶

$$\frac{5}{9} \div \frac{2}{3} = \frac{5}{9} \times \frac{3}{2} = \frac{15}{18} = \frac{15}{18} \div \frac{3}{3} = \frac{5}{6}$$

Keywords
- dividend
- quotient
- reciprocals

Math

6

Though this book was written more than 65 years ago, it will still interest readers today. I have always loved horses, so the friendship between Alec and the stallion really touched me. The character of Alec is well written, and the way Farley writes about the stallion is amazing. It's really hard to write well about animals, but Farley manages it.

I suggest that everyone, young and old, tries reading this book. I don't think anyone will regret it.

End with a recommendation about the book. Suggest the type of audience you think will enjoy it the most.

Movie and restaurant reviews work pretty much the same way as book reviews. They follow the same basic format.

Keywords
- review
- opinion
- book reviews
- plot

Adding and Subtracting Decimals

Decimals, like fractions, are pieces of a whole. You can use a number line to add or subtract decimals. What is the sum of $1.3 + 0.8$?

1.1 1.2 1.3 1.4 1.5 1.6 1.7 1.8 1.9 2.0 2.1 2.2 2.3

So $1.3 + 0.8 = 2.1$.

Add or subtract decimals just as you would whole numbers. First align the numbers by place value. Then add or subtract each place value from right to left, **regrouping** when needed. Remember to keep the decimal point in the same place in the answer.

Example 1: $5.2 + 0.98 + 3.15 = ?$

$$
\begin{array}{r}
{\scriptstyle 1\ 1} \\
5.2 \\
0.98 \\
+\,3.15 \\
\hline
9.33
\end{array}
$$

So $5.2 + 0.98 + 3.15 = 9.33$.

Example 2: $8.91 - 3.65 = ?$

$$
\begin{array}{r}
{\scriptstyle 8\ 11} \\
8.9\!\!\not{1} \\
-\,3.65 \\
\hline
5.26
\end{array}
$$

So $8.91 - 3.65 = 5.26$.

Estimate a sum or difference by rounding to the nearest whole numbers before finding the actual answer. If the estimate is close to the actual answer, then you know that your answer is reasonable.

$$
\begin{array}{r}
26.34 \longrightarrow 26 \\
-\,17.98 \longrightarrow -18 \\
\hline
8.36 \qquad\ \ 8
\end{array}
$$

8 is close to 8.36, so the answer is reasonable.

Keywords
- decimals
- regrouping
- estimate

Math

7

WRITING
Reviews

A **review** describes something you have read, seen, or experienced. It tells a little about the item and gives your **opinion** of it. The most common kinds of reviews are **book reviews**, movie reviews, and restaurant reviews.

Look at the following book review. It shows you a review's basic format.

A Special Friendship
by Justine Mack

Always identify the book's title and author in the first paragraph.

The Black Stallion, by Walter Farley, is one of my favorite books. This classic tale of the friendship between a boy and a horse has been popular for ages, with good reason. No one who reads the book can fail to be moved by the story.

Use this paragraph to give a brief summary of the book's **plot**. Be careful not to give too much away, and never reveal the ending!

Use this paragraph to give your opinion of the book. Try to back it up with reasons and details.

The Black Stallion is about a boy named Alec who loves to ride horses. The ship Alec is traveling on sinks, and a beautiful black stallion saves his life. Together, the two are stranded on a desert island. Slowly, a special bond builds between them. By the time Alec and the horse are rescued, they have become close companions. Alec goes on to ride the black stallion as a prizewinning jockey.

Multiplying Decimals

You **multiply decimals** the same way you multiply whole numbers. But you must be sure to place the decimal point correctly in the product. Count the number of places to the right of the decimal point in each factor and add them together. This is the number of places there will be to the right of the decimal point in the product.

Example 1

$$
\begin{array}{r}
\overset{2}{2.4} \leftarrow \text{1 decimal place} \\
\times \quad 5 \leftarrow \text{0 decimal places} \\
\hline
12.0 \leftarrow \text{1 decimal place}
\end{array}
$$

Example 2

$$
\begin{array}{r}
\overset{2}{2.4} \leftarrow \text{1 decimal place} \\
\times \ 0.5 \leftarrow \text{1 decimal place} \\
\hline
1.20 \leftarrow \text{2 decimal places}
\end{array}
$$

2.4 x 0.5 = ?

When you multiply a number by a decimal smaller than 1, the product will be smaller than that number. $6 \times 0.4 = 2.4$ (0.4 is smaller than 1; 2.4 is smaller than 6.)

Keywords
• multiply decimals

Math

8

*HELPSTER

WRITING
Literature Summaries

A **literature summary** is a brief rewording of the most important ideas in a story.
A good summary includes the setting, major characters, major **plot** events, and
theme of the story. It is concise but has all the important details. Use the following
chart to help you figure out what to include and, just as important, what to leave out.

Elements of a Literature Summary	
Major Characters	These include the main character or characters and any other characters that are important to the main plot. Any character involved in the main conflict or climax should be mentioned.
Setting	Include when and where the story takes place, if it is important to the story. If it's a contemporary story that could take place anywhere, the setting is less important.
Major Plot Events	Include the important events that surround the conflict, the climax, and the resolution. Don't include subplots or scenes or events that aren't related to, or important to, the conflict.
Theme	Include a brief statement about the story's theme.

Don't just copy passages from the story directly when you write your literature
summary. Instead, present your summary *in your own words*.

Keywords
- literature summary
- plot
- theme

Dividing Decimals

To divide a decimal by a whole number, place the **decimal point** for the **quotient** directly above the decimal point in the **dividend.** Then divide the same way you divide whole numbers.

Compare, divide, multiply, subtract, and bring down the next digit in the dividend.

LOOK at the divisor (4) and the first digit of the dividend (8).

THINK "What's $8 \div 4$?" ($8 \div 4 = 2$)

WRITE the partial quotient (2) above the dividend. Subtract.

Remember to put the decimal into your quotient.

$$
\begin{array}{r}
2.14 \\
4\overline{)8.56} \\
-8 \\
\hline
5 \\
-4 \\
\hline
16 \\
-16 \\
\hline
0
\end{array}
$$

If the **divisor** includes a decimal, count the number of digits to its right. Move the decimal of the quotient that many places to the *left*.

Keywords
- decimal point
- quotient
- dividend
- divisor

Math

✳HELPSTER

Compare-and-Contrast Essays

A **compare-and-contrast** essay compares two people, places, things, or ideas. It looks at how two subjects are both alike and different. It can be formatted two ways: **subject by subject** or **point by point**.

Essay: How Are Cats and Dogs Alike and Different?	
Subject by Subject	**Point by Point**
Introduction: Discuss both cats and dogs.	Introduction: Discuss both cats and dogs.
First few paragraphs: Discuss how cats look, act, and what they're like as pets.	First paragraph: Discuss the differences and similarities in how cats and dogs look.
Next few paragraphs: Discuss how dogs look, act, and what they're like as pets.	Second paragraph: Discuss the differences and similarities in how cats and dogs act.
Concluding paragraph: Summarize the differences and similarities between cats and dogs.	Third paragraph: Discuss the differences and similarities between cats and dogs as pets.
	Concluding paragraph: Summarize the differences and similarities between cats and dogs.

Make sure the subjects for your compare-and-contrast essay have something in common. You can compare two books or a book and a movie. It would be hard, however, to compare a book and shoe.

Keywords
- compare and contrast
- subject by subject
- point by point

Percent of a Number

Percent means "out of a hundred." 1% means "one out of a hundred" or "one hundredth." A percent can also be expressed as a **fraction** or as a **decimal**.

What is 30% as a fraction? As a decimal?

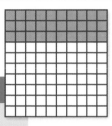

Write a Percent as a Fraction	Write a Percent as a Decimal
LOOK at the number before the % sign (30).	**LOOK** at the number before the % sign (30).
THINK "That's 30 hundredths."	**THINK** "That's 30 hundredths."
WRITE the number as the numerator and 100 as the denominator.	**WRITE** the number with the decimal point moved two places to the left.
$30\% = \frac{30}{100} = \frac{30 \div 10}{100 \div 10} = \frac{3}{10}$	$30\% = 30.0$
Remember to use the greatest common factor (GCF) to write your answer in simplest terms.	

$$30\% = \frac{3}{10} = 0.3$$

100% is the number 1 or one whole. 100% of any number is that number itself. 100% of 38 = 1×38 = 38.

50% of 200 = 0.5×200 = 100.   150% of 200 = 1.5×200 = 300.

Keywords
- percent
- fraction
- decimal

Math

10

✳HELPSTER

WRITING
Publishing

After working so hard, it's important to publish, or share, your **final draft**. Be sure to include any **graphics** you have chosen to use. Graphics are a great way to display information.

Also be sure to give your work a **title** that accurately summarizes what the work is about and to include your name on the front page or cover sheet. After all the sweat you put into it, you want to be sure to get credit.

Once your writing project is finished, you can share it in many ways, including:

▶ putting it in a binder and displaying it in class,

▶ having a publishing party,

▶ putting it up on the bulletin board,

▶ taking it home to share with friends and family,

▶ posting it on the Web through a personal or classroom Web site.

Way to go!

Cats Are
BETTER!
by
Julie Smith

If you want to post your work on the Web, make sure you ask your teacher if it's all right. Include your name and your school's name and address. If people see it and have questions, they can use that information to contact you. Do *not* post your home address or phone number.

Keywords
• final draft
• graphics
• title

✳**HELPSTER**

Fractions, Decimals, and Percents

Write a Decimal as a Percent

Write 0.62 as a percent.
Move the decimal point 2 places to the right.
0.62 ⟶ 62.
0.62 = 62%

Write a Fraction as a Percent

Write $\frac{3}{20}$ as a percent.
Divide to find an equivalent decimal.
$3 \div 20 = 0.15$
Then write the decimal as a percent.
0.15 = 15%
$\frac{3}{20} = 15\%$

Write a Decimal as a Fraction

Write 0.24 as a fraction.

LOOK at the last digit to the right of the decimal (4).
THINK "That's in the hundredths place."
WRITE that number (100) as your denominator. Use all digits without the decimal as your numerator.

$$0.24 = \frac{24}{100} = \frac{24 \div 4}{100 \div 4} = \frac{6}{25}$$

Remember to use the GCF (4) to write your answer in simplest terms.

Write a Fraction as a Decimal

Write $\frac{3}{8}$ as a decimal.

LOOK at the numerator (3) and the denominator (8).
THINK "Fractions are division problems. What is $3 \div 8$?"
WRITE out the division problem. The quotient will be a decimal.

$$\frac{3}{8} = 0.375$$

```
     0.375
8)3.000
  −24
   60
  −56
   40
  −40
    0
```

Keywords
- fraction
- decimal
- percent

Math

Using Proofreading Marks

You can use these **proofreading marks** symbols as you edit.

house
Cats make good ∧pets.

Cats don't make good pets.

When cats are happy, they purr and let you pet them. In conclusion, consider getting a cat.

Unlike dogs, cats don't require daily walking⊙

Cats are beautiful, friendly, and useful.

some people think cats are mean, but it isn't true.

Most people who have cats are very happy with them.

insert	∧
delete	℘
add comma	⌒
make lowercase	/ *lc*
begin new paragraph	#
add period	⊙
capitalize	☰ *CAP*
close up space	⌒

Look online to find a more complete listing of proofreading marks.

Keywords
• proofreading marks

Integers

Integers are the set of whole numbers, their opposites, and zero. The **opposite** of any number is the number that is the same distance from zero, but on the other side of zero on a number line.

Positive integers are numbers like 1, 2, 3 . . .
They are more than zero.

Negative integers are numbers like −1, −2, −3 . . .
They are less than zero.

Zero is neither positive nor negative.

Positive and negative integers are used to describe many situations. For example:

▶ + 60, or 60, can represent a temperature of 60°F above zero (warm) or 60 dollars ($60.00).

▶ −4 can represent a temperature of 4°F below zero (very cold) or a debt of 4 dollars (−$4.00).

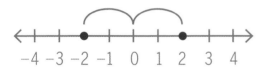

Negative integers tell you how much more of something you need to reach zero. If you have −$4.50 in a bank account, you need $4.50 more to break even. In other words, −$4.50 tells you that you owe $4.50. Once you pay it, you will have no money, or $0.00.

Keywords
- integers
- opposite
- positive integers
- negative integers
- zero

Math

12

WRITING
Editing

Editing is the next step after revising. When you edit, you make sure the words and sentences you use sound good. You also make sure that your grammar, spelling, and punctuation are correct. To edit, ask yourself the following questions:

▶ Does my writing sound good when I read it aloud?

▶ Have I used words correctly? Have I spelled words correctly?

▶ Have I used the correct grammar, capitalization, and punctuation?

▶ Is my handwriting or computer document legible?

Use a dictionary and a thesaurus to check your grammar, spelling, and word choices. You can also use your computer software's spell-checker and grammar check. These do not catch all mistakes, though, and sometimes find mistakes where there are none. And they can't know which homograph is correct for the context. Computer checks are no substitute for carefully rereading your own work.

Ask a friend or family member to help you edit and **proofread**. A fresh pair of eyes can sometimes catch mistakes you miss.

Keywords
• editing
• proofread

Absolute Value

The **absolute value** of an integer is its distance from zero on the number line.
Any number and its opposite have the same absolute value.
Zero has an absolute value of 0. Every other integer, positive or negative, has an absolute value greater than zero.

Absolute value is indicated by placing the number between two vertical lines:

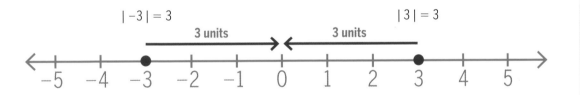

$|-3| = 3$ $|3| = 3$

3 units   3 units

You may see absolute value lines around a math problem.
Solve it and then find the absolute value of the answer.

$|7 - 10| = |-3| = 3$

Keywords
• absolute value

Math

13

WRITING
Revising

After finishing your first draft, the next step is to revise. **Revising** means going back to improve or correct parts of your draft. To revise your work, ask yourself these questions:

▶ Do my introduction and conclusion grab the reader's attention?

▶ Does everything make sense?

▶ Does the order of ideas and paragraphs seem logical?

▶ Do I support my ideas with facts and details?

▶ Have I included all the information I need?

▶ Do I go into enough detail about facts and ideas?

▶ Are my ideas presented clearly?

If you answer *no* to any of these questions, rewrite to fix the problem. You might need to add, delete, rewrite, or rearrange sentences and paragraphs. When you are almost done revising, consider showing your work to a friend or family member. Use his or her feedback to make your draft even better.

Your draft can be clear and well organized, but it still might be boring if you haven't varied your **sentence structure**. Make sure that the sentences in your work don't all begin the same way. Mix in short sentences with longer ones, complex sentences with simple ones. Also try to vary your vocabulary.

Keywords
• revising
• sentence structure

Adding and Subtracting Integers

▶ To add two **negative integers**, add them as though they were positive (add their **absolute values**) and then put a negative sign in front of the sum. A negative plus a negative = a negative.

▶ Adding a negative is the same as subtracting a positive: $10 + (-4) = 10 - 4 = 6$.

▶ Subtracting a negative is the same as adding a positive: $8 - (-3) = 8 + 3 = 11$.

▶ When you subtract a **positive integer** from a smaller positive integer, your answer (the difference) will be negative: $5 - 12 = -(12 - 5) = -7$.

Adding Two Negative Integers	Subtracting Two Negative Integers
$-5 + -6 = -(5 + 6) = -11$ $-8 + (-2) = -(8 + 2) = -10$	$-4 - (-2) = -4 + 2 = -2$ $-3 - (-5) = -3 + 5 = 2$
Adding with Different Signs	**Subtracting with Different Signs**
$-6 + 3 = 3 - 6 = -(6 - 3) = -3$ $4 + (-8) = 4 - 8 = -4$	$5 - (-4) = 5 + 4 = 9$ $(-2) - 6 = -2 + (-6) = -(2 + 6) = -8$

You can use a number line to add or subtract integers. Move right when you add a positive number (or subtract a negative). Move left when you subtract a positive number (or add a negative). The number line below shows $-3 + 2 = -1$.

Keywords
- negative integers
- absolute values
- positive integer

Math

14

WRITING
Drafting

Drafting means using the material you put together in the prewriting stage to write a first, or rough, draft. For this draft, don't worry very much about grammar, punctuation, and spelling. Instead, focus on the big picture. Make sure you include all the information you planned to use. A good **first draft** has the following:

▶ **A Thesis:** This is the central, or main, idea of your writing. All the other ideas in your writing are there to support the **thesis**.

▶ **More Than One Paragraph:** Each new paragraph is indented. Most paragraphs will have a topic sentence followed by sentences containing supporting facts, details, or explanations. Start a new paragraph when you introduce a new idea. Make sure to include **transitions**. Transitions connect a topic to the one that follows it. They make your writing flow from one paragraph to the next.

▶ **A Logical Sequence of Paragraphs:** The introduction, or introductory paragraph, states the thesis. Supporting paragraphs give details that support the thesis. The conclusion, or concluding paragraph, wraps things up.

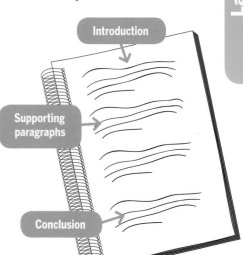

Introduction

Supporting paragraphs

Conclusion

Going back and rereading as you write your first draft will slow you down. You will have time later to revise. For now, just concentrate on getting all your information into your draft.

Keywords
• first draft
• thesis
• transitions

Exponents

Use **exponents** when you multiply a number by itself: $2 \times 2 = 2^2$ or "two squared."

$$2 \times 2 \times 2 \times 2 = 2^4.$$

In the expression 2^4, 2 is the **base** and 4 is the exponent.
This can be read as "two to the fourth **power**."

So $$2^4 = 2 \times 2 \times 2 \times 2 = 16.$$

Any number to the first power equals that number. Examples: $5^1 = 5$ and $200^1 = 200$.
Any non-zero number to the zero power equals one. Examples: $8^0 = 1$ and $46^0 = 1$.

To find the value of a number written with exponents, multiply the
base by itself the same number of times as shown by the exponent.

$3^3 = 3 \times 3 \times 3 = 27$

Keywords
• exponents
• base
• power

Math

15

WRITING
Prewriting

Writing a story, essay, or report is a process. Prewriting is the first step in that process. It's what you do even before you know what you are going to write. Below are some of the methods of prewriting.

Brainstorming	Asking Questions	Taking Notes	Using Graphic Organizers	Keeping a Log	Creating a Simple Outline
Brainstorming means making a list of everything that comes to mind about a particular topic. Don't stop to think about whether the ideas are good or bad. Just write them down.	All good essays and research papers start with a question. Make a list of all the questions you have about your topic. Include every question, no matter how silly you think it is. Then use the list to help you narrow your topic.	Taking notes is a useful prewriting tool for a research report. As you do research, take notes on what you find. Later, you can organize the notes before you begin writing.	Graphic organizers can help you organize your thoughts about a topic. They are useful for stories and essays with assigned topics. **Time lines, character webs,** and **charts** can help you get organized.	Keeping a log is a good prewriting tool for stories and essays. Record your thoughts and observations in the log over several days. Then look back over what you have written.	Make a simple outline that includes all the points you would like to make about a topic. Then assess your outline. What information do you still need to get?

Keywords
- time lines
- character webs
- charts

Base 10

A **power** is another name for an exponent. "10 to the third power" $= 10^3 = 1,000$. Our number system is based on powers of 10. Each digit of a number is worth 10 times the digit to its right.
The **metric system** also uses powers of 10 (or **base 10**).

1 kilometer $= 10^3$ meters $= 1,000$ m.
1 meter $= 10^2$ centimeters $= 100$ cm.
1 centimeter $= 10^1$ millimeters $= 10$ mm.

In base 10, the exponent is the same as the number of zeros in the value of the expression.		
$10^5 = 10 \times 10 \times 10 \times 10 \times 10$	$= 100,000$	⟵ 5 zeros
$10^4 = 10 \times 10 \times 10 \times 10$	$= 10,000$	⟵ 4 zeros
$10^3 = 10 \times 10 \times 10$	$= 1,000$	⟵ 3 zeros
$10^2 = 10 \times 10$	$= 100$	⟵ 2 zeros
$10^1 = 10$	$= 10$	⟵ 1 zero
$10^0 = 1$		⟵ no zeros

Scientific notation makes it easy to write large numbers. For example, light travels at a speed of about 18,000,000,000 (18 billion) meters per minute. Scientists write this number as 1.8×10^{10}. This is the same as multiplying $1.8 \times 10 \times 10 \times 10 \times 10 \times 10 \times 10 \times 10 \times 10 \times 10 \times 10$.

Keywords
- power
- metric system
- base 10
- scientific notation

Math

*HELPSTER

16

WRITING
Writing Process Flowchart

Follow these steps to becoming a great writer. (Learn more about them on the following pages.)

1. **Prewriting**

2. **Drafting**

3. **Revising**

4. **Proofreading**

5. **Publishing**

Primes, Composites, and Factors

A factor is a number that is multiplied to give a product.

Example: $4 \times 3 = 12$ $6 \times 2 = 12$ $12 \times 1 = 12$

4, 3, 6, 2, 12, and 1 are factors of 12.

A **prime number** is a whole number greater than 1 that has only two factors: itself and one.
Example: $1 \times 13 = 13$ No other whole numbers multiply to make 13.

So 13 is a prime number, because it has only two factors: 1 and 13.

A **composite number** is a whole number that has more than two factors.
Example: $1 \times 14 = 14$ $2 \times 7 = 14$

So 14 is a composite number, because it has 1, 2, 7, and 14 as factors.

The number 2 is the only even prime number. Every **even number** greater than 2 is composite because it has at least three factors: 1, 2, and the number itself. However, not every **odd number** is a prime. For example, 25 is odd but it has 1, 5, and 25 as factors.

Keywords
- prime number
- composite number
- even number
- odd number

Math

*HELPSTER

17

Literary Devices

Poets and story writers often use **literary devices**, known as figurative language, to liven up their writing. Some devices focus on sound. Others create a comparison or an image in the reader's mind. Here are some common ones.

Literary Device	What It Is	Examples
Simile	a comparison of two unlike things using the words *like* or *as*	In his sweater, hat, and booties, the dog looked like a little old man. The dog was as big as a racehorse.
Metaphor	a comparison of two unlike things that describes one thing as if it were another without using the words *like* or *as*	The dog was a runaway train, hurtling toward me out of control.
Alliteration	the repetition of consonant sounds at the beginning of words	When the pretty poodles pranced and paraded, their pompous owner puffed up with pride.
Onomatopoeia	using words that imitate sounds	All the dogs were barking—*yap, ruff, arf!*
Hyperbole	unrealistic exaggeration	That dog is so smart he can read the newspaper!
Symbolism	using a word or an object to create a mental picture of something else	As the flag waved in the breeze, he thought of parades, fireworks, and the Fourth of July.
Imagery	descriptive writing that appeals to one or more of the five senses	Ike heard the laughter from the kitchen and smelled the bread baking. He pictured the table, worn smooth through years of use. He could already taste the warm, buttery treat.

Prime Factorization

You can express any number as the product of **prime factors**.

You can use a **factor tree** to find the prime factors of a number.

Even though a number may have several different factors, those factors can be reduced to the same prime factors.

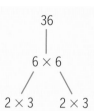

Example:

$$36$$
$$4 \times 9$$
$$2 \times 2 \qquad 3 \times 3$$

$36 = 2 \times 2 \times 3 \times 3$, or $36 = 2^2 \times 3^2$.

$$36$$
$$6 \times 6$$
$$2 \times 3 \qquad 2 \times 3$$

$36 = 2 \times 3 \times 2 \times 3$, or $36 = 2^2 \times 3^2$.

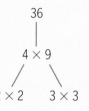

Put the prime factors of each number in order from smallest to greatest.

Use **exponents** when a prime factor appears more than once.

$12 = 3 \times 2 \times 2 = 2^2 \times 3$

Keywords
• prime factors
• factor tree
• exponents

Math

18

*HELPSTER

READING
More Reading Comprehension Tips

Here are additional reading skills you can use to make sure you understand the nonfiction texts that you read.

Reading Skill	What It Is / How It Works
Identifying **cause and effect**	An effect is what happens. A cause is what makes it happen and is sometimes *why* it happens. As you read, look for causes that can explain events. Also look for the effects of events.
Comparing and contrasting	To compare, think about the ways two or more things are alike. To contrast, think about how they differ.
Asking questions	After reading, it's important to think about what was not said as well as what was said. Make a list of questions about the topic that your reading did not answer. Then think of places where you might find answers to your questions.
Using visual information	In nonfiction, most visuals have a purpose. Charts, graphs, and diagrams can supply detailed information to support statements in the text. Photos and illustrations can help you understand and visualize the material being presented.

Captions are separate text that goes with the graphics. They often give additional information that does not fit into the main text. To get the most out of your reading, make sure that you look at all the visuals and read all captions carefully.

Keywords
- cause and effect
- comparing and contrasting

✳HELPSTER

Greatest Common Factor

The greatest **factor** of two or more numbers is called the **greatest common factor (GCF)**.
To find the greatest common factor of two or more numbers, list the factors of each number.
Then circle the factors that the numbers have in common and find which of these is the greatest.

Example: What is the greatest common factor of 30 and 45?

Factors of 30: 1, 2, 3, 5, 6, 10, 15, 30   Factors of 45: 1, 3, 5, 9, 15, 45

The common factors are 1, 3, 5, and 15.

The greatest common factor is 15.

To find the factors of a number, set up a
table and begin with the number 1. Find its
partner (the quotient when you divide the
original number by that factor). Continue up,
deciding whether each number (2, 3, 4, etc.)
is a factor and what its partner is.

Factors of 24		
1	24	← $1 \times 24 = 24$
2	12	← $2 \times 12 = 24$
3	8	← $3 \times 8 = 24$
4	6	← $4 \times 6 = 24$

Keywords
• factor
• greatest common factor (GCF)

Math

19

HELPSTER

Reading Comprehension Tips

It's important to be able to understand and analyze the nonfiction texts that you read. You can use the reading skills on this page and the next one to help you do that.

Reading Skill	What It Is / How It Works
Finding the **main idea**	The main idea is the most important idea in a text. It can be stated or unstated. Ask yourself: What is the most important idea in what I am reading?
Rereading	Rereading is a useful tool for difficult texts. If you don't understand something the first time, go back and read it again. Try rereading with a specific question in mind. As you reread, look for the answer.
Making **inferences**	An inference is a logical guess about something that is not stated. To make an inference, use clues in the text to figure out something that has not been told.
Drawing **conclusions**	A conclusion is a logical decision that readers make based upon what they know and what they read. Draw conclusions by combining what you already know with what you read to form a complete picture.
Paraphrasing	Paraphrasing means putting what you read into your own words. It helps you evaluate your comprehension. If you can clearly paraphrase what you've read, you probably understand it.

Headings and subheadings often give clues to the main idea presented in a chapter or a section of a book or an article. In nonfiction, some tables of contents also summarize the main points that are covered in each chapter.

Keywords
- main idea
- inferences
- conclusions
- paraphrasing

*HELPSTER

Multiples and Least Common Multiples

When you count by a number, you name its **multiples**. 3, 6, 9, 12, 15 . . . are the multiples of 3. You can also multiply a number by 1, 2, 3, and so on to find multiples of a number.

List the first six multiples of 12.

1 × 12	2 × 12	3 × 12	4 × 12	5 × 12	6 × 12
12	24	36	48	60	72

A **common multiple** is a number that is a multiple of two or more numbers.
The **least common multiple (LCM)** is the smallest multiple that those numbers have in common.

What is the least common multiple of 6 and 9?

Multiples of 6: 6, 12, ⑱, 24, 30, ㊱, 42, 48, (54), 60, 66, (72)
Multiples of 9: 9, ⑱, 27, ㊱, 45, (54), 63, (72)

18, 36, 54, and 72 are all common multiples of 6 and 9.
However, 18 is the least common multiple of 6 and 9.

You can use **prime factors** to find least common multiples.
What is the LCM of 8 and 28? First find the prime factors of each number.
$8 = 2 \times 2 \times 2$ $28 = 2 \times 2 \times 7$
$2 \times 2 \times 2 \times 7 = 8 \times 7 = 56$, so 56 is the least common multiple of 8 and 28.

Keywords
- multiples
- common multiple
- least common multiple (LCM)
- prime factors

READING
Point of View, Nonfiction

Point of view in nonfiction is more complicated than in fiction. It has to do with how an author's **perspective** influences her or his writing. Here are some of the key things to consider when you weigh an author's perspective.

▶ **Opinions:** What does the author believe? Is the author of an essay on dogs a dog lover or a dog hater? Is she or he trying to be truly objective or neutral?

▶ **Background:** What is the author's background? Our background and experiences can color how we see the world and how we judge the actions of others. Did the author live through a war? Did he or she have a difficult home life as a child? Depending upon the author's topic or purpose, such experiences can influence his or her writing.

▶ **Era:** When did the author write? People in some past eras had different values and beliefs than we have today. Nonfiction from those eras may reflect this.

▶ **Age:** How old is the author? Young people and old people often see things from different points of view.

▶ **Economic Class:** Is the writer wealthy or poor? How much money people have can influence their opinions.

Before you read an author's work, look at the biographical information about him or her on the book cover or at the end of the article. Sometimes that will give you clues to the author's point of view on the topic at hand.

Keywords
• point of view
• nonfiction
• perspective

Square Numbers

If you multiply a whole number greater than 0 by itself, the product is called a **square number**. It is also called the "square" of the original number.

You can also say the original number was "squared." For example: 2 "squared" = 4; 3 "squared" = 9.

$1 \times 1 = \mathbf{1}$ $2 \times 2 = \mathbf{4}$

$3 \times 3 = \mathbf{9}$ $4 \times 4 = \mathbf{16}$

$5 \times 5 = \mathbf{25}$ $6 \times 6 = \mathbf{36}$

A square number is the same as writing the number as a **base** with the **exponent** 2.

For example: $2^2 = 2 \times 2 = 4$; $3^2 = 3 \times 3 = 9$; $4^2 = 4 \times 4 = 16$.

Keywords
- square number
- base
- exponent

Math

21

HELPSTER

Point of View, Fiction

I want to complain to the cook!

Whenever you read something, it's important to keep in mind the **point of view** of the person narrating it. This is true in both fiction and nonfiction. Here, take a look at how point of view works in fiction. On the next page, see how it influences nonfiction.

In fiction, there are two main points of view.

First Person	Third Person
▶ The story is narrated by one of the characters.	▶ The story is narrated by someone outside the story—the author.
▶ The pronoun *I* is used.	▶ Third-person pronouns are used.
▶ Often, the **first-person narrator** is the main character. Sometimes, it is another character in the story.	▶ An all-knowing **third-person narrator** knows the thoughts, feelings, and actions of every character in a story.
▶ When reading a story with a first-person point of view, keep in mind that the character who is narrating may not always be telling the truth. The narrator's thoughts and opinions influence what he or she chooses to tell.	▶ A limited third-person narrator knows only the thoughts, feelings, and actions of one character or several characters.

Keywords
- point of view
- first-person narrator
- third-person narrator

Sometimes the title of a book or an article will give you a clue to the point of view that is used. *My Life as a Dog Washer* is probably written in the first person. *How Hank Lost and Found His Dog* is probably written in the third person.

Long Division

Long division can help you figure out how many times one number fits into another. $114 \div 6 = ?$

STEP ONE

$$\begin{array}{r} 1 \\ 6\overline{)114} \\ -6\downarrow \\ \hline 54 \end{array}$$

LOOK at the **divisor** (6) and the first digit of the **dividend** (1). 1 is smaller than 6, so look at the first two digits: 11.

THINK "How many times does 6 fit into 11? 1 time."

WRITE the partial **quotient** (1) above the dividend and the product of the divisor and the partial quotient ($6 \times 1 = 6$) under the dividend. Subtract and write the difference below ($11 - 6 = 5$). Bring down the next digit of the dividend (4).

STEP TWO

$$\begin{array}{r} 19 \\ 6\overline{)114} \\ -6\downarrow \\ \hline 54 \\ -54 \\ \hline 0 \end{array}$$

→ Align the partial quotient (9) with the last number you brought down (4).

→ When you've brought down all digits in the dividend (114), this number (0) is the **remainder**.

LOOK at the divisor (6) and the difference (54).

THINK "How many times does 6 fit into 54? 9 times."

WRITE the partial quotient (9) above the dividend, and the product of the divisor and the new partial quotient ($6 \times 9 = 54$) under it. Subtract and write the difference ($54 - 54 = 0$) below.

Answer: 19 with a remainder of 0. (There is no remainder.)

Check your division with the **inverse operation**: multiplication. If the product of the divisor and the quotient is the dividend, your answer is correct: $6 \times 19 = 114$.

Keywords
- long division
- divisor
- dividend
- quotient
- remainder
- inverse operation

Math

✳HELPSTER

22

Fact Versus Opinion

Most nonfiction works contain both **facts** and **opinions**. It's important to be able to tell them apart. Here's how.

▶ Fact: a statement that can be proven true.
There are more than 150 recognized breeds of dogs.

▶ Opinion: a statement of what someone thinks, feels, or believes. It often contains signal words such as *think, believe, feel, best, worst, most, least.*
I think dogs make much better pets than cats do.

Good arguments use facts to support opinions. A reader can draw a **supported inference** from a good argument. Check out these examples of good and bad persuasion.

Good Argument

Dogs have a herd instinct that makes them loyal to their owners. They are also protectors, since most dogs bark if strangers are around. If properly trained, dogs are also obedient. All these things make dogs a superior pet.

The writer lists facts to support the opinion.

The writer's final inference is based on facts.

Bad Argument

Dogs are the most beautiful animals in the world. They are also the most fun. When I am with my dog, I am as happy as a person can be. No other pet makes me feel that way. That's why I know dogs are a superior pet.

This writer simply lists a series of opinions. The final inference is not supported by any facts.

Persuasive language often presents opinions as facts. When looking at ads or other persuasive texts, ask yourself: Can the statements made be proven true? Are the statements presenting an opinion as a fact?

Keywords
• facts
• opinions
• supported inference

MEASUREMENT
Length and Perimeter

Length is the distance from one end of a line segment to the other end. **Perimeter** is the distance around a figure. You can also think of perimeter as the sum of the lengths of all sides of a shape.

You can use **metric** or **customary units** to measure length and perimeter.

Metric Units of Length	Customary Units of Length
1 centimeter (cm) = 10 millimeters (mm)	1 foot (ft.) = 12 inches (in.)
1 decimeter (dm) = 10 centimeters (cm)	1 yard (yd.) = 3 feet (ft.)
1 meter (m) = 100 centimeters (cm)	1 mile (mi.) = 5,280 feet (ft.)
1 kilometer (km) = 1,000 meters (m)	1 mile (mi.) = 1,760 yards (yd.)

Perimeter of triangle

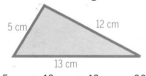

5 cm + 12 cm + 13 cm = 30 cm

Perimeter of rectangle

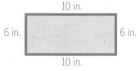

2 × (10 in. + 6 in.) = 32 in.

Perimeter of square

4 × 9 mm = 36 mm

Learning these prefixes can help you memorize metric measurements:

milli- = thousandth   1 millimeter = $\frac{1}{1,000}$ of a meter

centi- = hundredth   1 centimeter = $\frac{1}{100}$ of a meter

deci- = tenth   1 decimeter = $\frac{1}{10}$ of a meter

kilo- = thousand   1 kilometer = 1,000 meters

Keywords
- length
- perimeter
- metric units
- customary units

Math

23

✳HELPSTER

READING
Reading Nonfiction

Nonfiction works are often organized in ways that make them easy to read and use. Look for these features of nonfiction books and articles.

Feature	What It Is	Where to Find It
Table of contents	Lists chapter titles, article titles, and their beginning pages	Near the very front of a book or magazine
Headings and subheadings	These are titles that divide text. They give readers clues about what will follow.	Throughout books and magazine articles
Graphics	The photographs, illustrations, maps, charts, and graphs in a book or an article	Throughout books and magazine articles
Glossary	Gives definitions for important words used in a book or an article	Near the back of a book or toward the end of an article
Index	Alphabetically lists all the subjects discussed in a book	At the back of a book
Footnotes or endnotes	List sources that the author used. They also often include extra information. Footnotes and endnotes are usually numbered.	Footnotes are at the bottom of page; endnotes are at the back of a book.

Preview a book by looking at its features. First look at the table of contents and the index. Then thumb through and look at the headings and graphics.

Keywords
- table of contents
- headings and subheadings
- graphics
- glossary
- index
- footnotes or endnotes

✳HELPSTER

Weight and Mass

A scale is used to measure the **weight**, or heaviness, of an object.
It can also measure the **mass**, or amount of matter, in an object.

In **customary units**, weight is measured in ounces, pounds, and tons.

1 pound (lb.) = 16 ounces (oz.)
1 ton (t.) = 2,000 pounds (lb.)

1 ounce   1 pound   1 ton

In **metric units**, mass is measured in grams, kilograms, and metric tons.

1 kilogram (kg) = 1,000 grams (g)
1 metric ton (t) = 1,000 kilograms (kg)

1 gram   1 kilogram   1 metric ton

1 cubic centimeter of water (enough water to fill a cube with sides 1 cm long; 1 milliliter of water) has a mass of 1 gram.

Math

Keywords
- weight
- mass
- customary units
- metric units

24

READING
More About Plot

The **plot** of a story has three important parts: the **conflict**, the **climax**, and the **resolution**.

▶ The conflict is the central problem in the story. There are two types of conflict.

1. In *internal conflicts*, characters struggle with important feelings or decisions.
2. In *external conflicts*, characters struggle with other characters or against nature.

Although a story always has one central conflict, complex stories may also have other, lesser conflicts.

▶ The climax is the point in the plot when the main character realizes how to resolve the conflict.

▶ The resolution is when a solution to the climax, or problem, is reached. This comes at the end of the plot.

Often, a plot is organized in time order, or chronological order. That means events are written about in the order in which they happen.

Keywords
- plot
- conflict
- climax
- resolution

Time

Time is measured in seconds, minutes, and hours.
There are **analog** and **digital** clocks and watches.
SAY "Nine ten" or "ten minutes after nine." ————————➤

Elapsed time is the amount of time that passes from the start of an event to the end of an event. The two clocks below show the time a movie started and the time it ended. How long did the movie last?

First count by hours, then count by minutes:
>   2:15 to 3:15 ←— 1 hour
>   3:15 to 4:15 ←— 1 hour
>   4:15 to 4:25 ←— 10 minutes

So the movie lasted 2 hours and 10 minutes.

You can also determine elapsed time by subtracting the start time from the end time. Remember when renaming hours as minutes that 1 hour = 60 minutes.

Start time: 6:48   End time: 9:20

$$9:20 \longleftarrow 9\text{ h. }20\text{ min. } = 8\text{ h. }80\text{ min.}$$
$$6:48 \longleftarrow -6\text{ h. }48\text{ min.} \quad -6\text{ h. }48\text{ min.}$$
$$\overline{\qquad\qquad\qquad\qquad 2\text{ h. }32\text{ min.}}$$

Keywords
• analog
• digital
• elapsed time

Math

25

Reading Fiction: The Elements of a Story

All fiction, whether it is realistic or unrealistic, has the same basic elements.

Characters	The characters are the people, animals, or imaginary beings that are in the story. The main character is the most important character in the story. Some stories have more than one main character.
Setting	The setting is where and when the story takes place. The story can be set in the real world or in an imaginary world, or sometimes in both. It can take place in the past, present, future, or, in the case of time-travel stories, all three.
Plot	The plot is what happens in the story. For more about plot, see the next page.
Theme	The theme is the important message or idea about life that a writer conveys through the story. The theme is almost never stated. Readers must figure it out for themselves. Usually, the story's conflict is closely related to the theme.
Mood	The mood is the overall feeling of a story. All the elements of a story contribute to its mood, but the setting, plot, and theme are the most important. A story's mood can be gloomy, sad, serious, lighthearted, scary, a combination of those, or anything in between. To figure out a story's mood, think about how you felt while you were reading it.

Keywords
- characters
- setting
- plot
- theme
- mood

Temperature

You can use a **thermometer** to measure **temperature** in **degrees Fahrenheit** (°F) or **degrees Celsius** (°C).

Degrees Fahrenheit are customary units of measure.
WRITE 25°F.
SAY "Twenty-five degrees Fahrenheit."

Degrees Celsius are metric units of measure.
WRITE −4°C.
SAY "Negative four degrees Celsius" or "four degrees below zero Celsius."

You can use the benchmark temperatures shown on the thermometer to determine whether a given temperature is cold, warm, or hot.

Keywords
- thermometer
- temperature
- degrees Fahrenheit (°F)
- degrees Celsius (°C)

Math

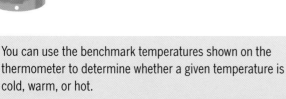

READING
Genres

Books come in many different **genres**, or types. Some are **fiction**, or made-up stories. Others are **nonfiction**, about things that are real.

Genre	Fiction or Nonfiction?/ Realistic or Not?	Example
Realistic fiction	fiction / realistic	*Brian's Winter* by Gary Paulsen
Mystery	fiction / realistic	*Chasing Vermeer* by Blue Balliett
Historical fiction	fiction / realistic	*The True Confessions of Charlotte Doyle* by Avi
Fantasy	fiction / unrealistic	*Harry Potter and the Sorcerer's Stone* by J. K. Rowling
Science fiction	fiction / unrealistic	*Out of the Silent Planet* by C. S. Lewis
Folktales (including myths, legends, fables, fairy tales, and tall tales)	fiction / unrealistic	*Shadow Spinner* by Susan Fletcher
Biography	nonfiction / realistic	*Genius: A Photobiography of Albert Einstein* by Marfe Ferguson Delano

Need a good book to read for an assignment? Ask your friends or teachers for recommendations. Many libraries have reading lists as well. You can also find reading lists and recommendations online.

Keywords
• genres
• fiction
• nonfiction

HELPSTER

Money

To find the total value of a collection of money: First find the total value of the **bills**.
Then find the total value of the **coins**. Remember: $1.00 = 4 quarters = 10 dimes = 20 nickels = 100 pennies.
Starting with the bill with the greatest value, count up.

$20.00	$30.00	$35.00	$41.00	$41.25	$41.60	$41.75	$41.76
		$40.00		$41.50	$41.70		

A scarf costs $14.73. Jennifer gives the clerk a $20 bill. What is her change?
Starting with the cost of the scarf, count up until you reach the total amount Jennifer gave the clerk.

COST				**Total change: $5.27**
$14.73	$14.74	$15.00	$20.00	
	$14.75			

You can subtract the cost from the amount paid to
find the amount of change. Subtract as you would
whole numbers, and then place the decimal point
and dollar sign in your answer.

$$\begin{array}{r} \overset{\scriptstyle 9\ 9}{1\ \cancel{10}\cancel{10}10} \\ \$\cancel{2}0.00 \\ -\ 14.73 \\ \hline \$5.27 \end{array}$$

Keywords
• bills
• coins

Subject-Verb Agreement

In sentences, the subject and verb must agree in number. That means that **singular** subjects take singular verbs and **plural** subjects take plural verbs.

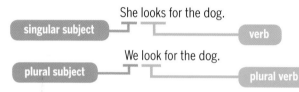

She looks for the dog.

singular subject — verb

We look for the dog.

plural subject — plural verb

Sometimes, it's harder to tell whether a subject is singular or plural. For example, some subjects are **compound subjects**. More than one noun forms the subject. Look at these examples.

What Kind of Compound Subject?	Is It Singular or Plural?	Examples
subjects using *and*	plural	Hank <u>and</u> I <u>wash</u> the dog. Rufus <u>and</u> Hank <u>run</u> around the yard.
subjects using *or*, *either / or*, *neither / nor*	singular	Sometimes, Hank <u>or</u> Rufus <u>runs</u> away. <u>Neither</u> Hank <u>nor</u> Rufus likes bath time.

The subject is often separated from the verb in a sentence. Always identify the subject and verb to make sure they agree. Example: A bucket of suds sits outside on the driveway. *Bucket*, the subject, is singular. *Of suds* is a prepositional phrase modifying *bucket*. Use a singular verb.

Keywords
- subject-verb agreement
- singular
- plural
- compound subjects

Lines and Rays

A **line** goes on forever in two directions.

WRITE $\overleftrightarrow{AB}$
SAY "Line AB."

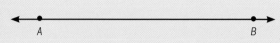

A **ray** has one endpoint and continues forever in one direction.

WRITE $\overrightarrow{CD}$.
SAY "Ray CD."

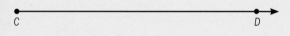

A **line segment** is a part of a line with two endpoints. Lines, rays, and line segments are straight. They do not curve.

WRITE $\overline{EF}$.
SAY "Line segment EF."

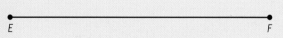

Parallel lines are lines that stay the same distance apart and never meet.

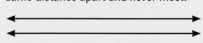

Perpendicular lines meet or cross at right angles.

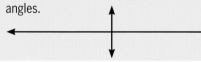

Keywords
- line
- ray
- line segment
- parallel lines
- perpendicular lines

When naming a ray, the first letter is always the endpoint.

Math

Interjections

An **interjection** is a word or phrase added to a sentence to express emotion.

> Oh, no! The dog just ran away!

interjection

An interjection often is followed by an **exclamation point**. However, if writers don't want to express such strong emotion, the interjection may be followed by a comma.

> Oh, my! Did you see that big bear?
> Oh, my, did you see that big bear?

Interjections are rarely used in formal writing, unless they are part of a quotation. Here are some common interjections in English: *oh, ouch, whoa, wow, hey, yes, no, alas.*

The word *interjection* comes from the Latin *inter*, meaning "among, between," and *iacere*, meaning "throw." It is a word or phrase "thrown into" the rest of the sentence.

Keywords
- interjection
- exclamation point

*HELPSTER

Angles

Angles are formed when two rays, lines, or line segments meet at a point called the **vertex**.

You can use a **protractor** to measure an angle.

WRITE $\angle B$, $\angle ABC$

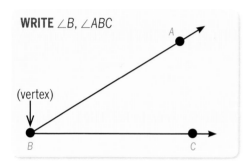

(vertex)

WRITE $m\angle RNM = 50°$

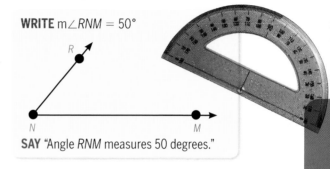

SAY "Angle *RNM* measures 50 degrees."

Learn the names of these angles.

An **acute angle** measures less than 90°.

A **right angle** measures 90°.

An **obtuse angle** measures more than 90° but less than 180°.

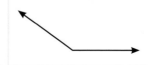

Keywords
- angles
- vertex
- protractor
- acute angle
- right angle
- obtuse angle

Math

Clauses

Clauses, like phrases, are groups of words. However, unlike phrases, clauses contain both a subject and a predicate. There are two types of clauses.

Type	Definition	Example
Independent clause	Contains a complete thought. Can be a sentence.	I was washing the dog.
Dependent clause	Does not contain a complete thought. Cannot be a sentence on its own.	While I was washing the dog

▶ Dependent clauses usually start with a **subordinating conjunction** and may begin with these words: *because, since, so, although, though, as, while, after, if, unless, until, when, before.*

▶ Use a dependent clause to give information that is less important than the information in an independent clause.

dependent clause   While I was washing the dog, he got loose and ran away.   **independent clause**

(In this sentence, the information about washing the dog is not as important as the fact that the dog ran away. So the information about washing the dog is presented in a dependent clause.)

Remember that a dependent clause *depends* on another clause to give it meaning and context. A dependent clause is also called a **subordinate clause**.

Keywords
- independent clause
- dependent clause
- subordinating conjunction
- subordinate clause

Polygons

A **polygon** is a closed figure made up of straight line segments.
Polygons are identified by the number of sides and **angles** they have.

 Triangle   **Quadrilateral**   **Pentagon**   **Hexagon**   **Octagon**

Polygons can be **regular** or **irregular**. If all the sides have equal lengths and all the
angles have equal measures, the polygon is regular. The quadrilateral shown above is irregular.
The triangle shown above is regular. It has equal sides and angles. It is called an **equilateral** triangle.

Regular polygons   **Irregular polygons**

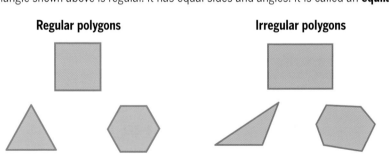

Keywords
- polygon
- angles
- triangle
- quadrilateral
- pentagon
- hexagon
- octagon
- regular
- irregular
- equilateral

Math

If a figure has a curved side, it is not a polygon.

HELPSTER

Prepositional Phrases

Prepositions are words that introduce and link nouns or pronouns to other words in a sentence. They often help to answer the questions When? and Where?

The word or phrase that the preposition introduces is known as the **object of the preposition**. The preposition and its object are together known as a **prepositional phrase**.

To identify a prepositional phrase, look for a phrase that beings with a preposition.

> **prepositional phrase**
>
> We found Rufus at the neighbor's house.
>
> **preposition**   **object of the preposition**

The following prepositional phrase is part of a **noun phrase**.
That means it modifies the noun.

> **noun phrase**
>
> The dog in the street barked loudly.
>
> **prepositional phrase**

Prepositional phrases that tell *when* begin with words such as *before*, *after*, *during*, *since*, and *until*. Those that tell *where* begin with words such as *above*, *below*, *in*, *out*, *at*, *around*, *across*, *through*, *under*, *up*, and *over*.

Keywords
- prepositions
- object of a preposition
- prepositional phrase
- noun phrase

Quadrilaterals

A **quadrilateral** is a polygon with four sides and four angles. There are different kinds of quadrilaterals.

 Quadrilateral   **Parallelogram**   **Rhombus**   **Rectangle**   **Square**   **Trapezoid**

What is the sum of the angle measures of a square?

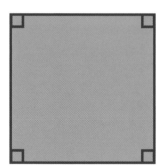

You know that a square has four right angles and a right angle measures 90°.

$4 \times 90° = 360°$

The sum of the measures of the angles of any quadrilateral is 360°.

A square is a parallelogram because it has two pairs of parallel sides. It is also a rectangle because it has four right angles. And it is a rhombus because it is a parallelogram with four sides of equal length.

Keywords
- quadrilateral
- parallelogram
- rhombus
- rectangle
- square
- trapezoid

Math

✳HELPSTER

Appositives

Appositives are nouns or pronouns—or noun phrases—that help to describe or explain another noun or pronoun. The appositive phrases in these sentences are underlined.

> Rufus, <u>our lovable dog</u>, has disappeared.
> The book <u>*How to Train Your Dog*</u> is helping me to control Rufus.

Here are the rules for using **commas** with appositives.

1. If the information in the appositive is essential to the sentence, *don't* set the appositive off with commas. Here, the name "Julia" is essential because it tells which of Hank's friends we're talking about.

> Hank's friend <u>Julia</u> has two dogs.

2. If the information in the appositive is not essential to the sentence, then set the appositive off with commas. Here, removing "Julia" or "a frisky fellow" would not change the meaning of the sentence. It is not essential information.

> Hank and his best friend, <u>Julia</u>, love dogs.
> Rufus, <u>a frisky fellow</u>, likes to run away.

Using an appositive is a useful way to combine two sentences.
Rufus is a dog. Hank and I own him. ▶ Hank and I own Rufus, <u>a dog</u>.
(The information from the first sentence has been turned into an appositive.)

Keywords
• appositives
• commas

Triangles

A triangle is a polygon with three sides and three angles.
There are different kinds of triangles.

 Equilateral   **Isosceles**   **Acute**   **Right**   **Scalene**   **Obtuse**

What is the missing angle measure?

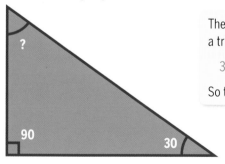

The sum of the measures of the interior angles of a triangle is 180°.

$$30° + 90° = 120° \qquad 180° - 120° = 60°$$

So the measure of the missing angle is 60°.

Remember: An acute triangle has three acute angles.
An obtuse triangle has one obtuse angle.
The sides and angles of a scalene triangle are each a different size.

Keywords
- equilateral triangle
- isosceles triangle
- acute triangle
- right triangle
- scalene triangle
- obtuse triangle

Math

*HELPSTER

Conjunctions

Conjunctions are words that link two separate words, phrases, or clauses.
There are three types of conjunctions: coordinating, subordinating, and correlative.

▶ Use **coordinating conjunctions** to join two words or ideas of equal importance. When coordinating
conjunctions connect two independent clauses, they turn them into a compound sentence.

Common Coordinating Conjunctions	Example Sentences
and, but, for, or, yet, so	Hank <u>and</u> I own the dog. I washed the dog, <u>so</u> he is really clean. Rufus is a good dog, <u>but</u> sometimes he runs away.

▶ Use **subordinating conjunctions** to join two ideas of unequal importance, such as a
dependent clause and an independent clause.

Common Subordinating Conjunctions	Example Sentences
because, since, so, although, though, as, while, after, if, unless, until, when, before	I had to wash the dog <u>because</u> he was so dirty. <u>Although</u> Hank claims to hate dogs, I know he really loves Rufus.

▶ **Correlative conjunctions** work only in pairs. Use them to join words or
phrases of equal importance.

Common Correlative Conjunctions	Example Sentences
both/and, either/or, neither/nor, not only/but also, whether/or	<u>Both</u> Hank <u>and</u> I take care of the dog. <u>Neither</u> Hank <u>nor</u> I could find Rufus.

Keywords
- conjunctions
- coordinating conjunctions
- subordinating conjunctions
- correlative conjunctions

Circles

A **circle** is a two-dimensional (flat) shape made by connecting all points located a certain distance from another point (the center of the circle).

The **radius** is a line segment from the center of a circle to any point on the circle.

The **diameter** is a line segment that connects two points on a circle and passes through its center.

The length of the diameter of a circle is always twice the length of the radius. The length of the radius of a circle is half of the length of the diameter.

Keywords
- circle
- radius
- diameter

Math

33

Adverbs

Adverbs are words that modify, or describe, verbs and adjectives. Most adverbs describe how, when, or where something is done.

How	slowly	I washed the dog <u>slowly</u>.
When	early	I washed the dog <u>early</u>.
Where	here	I washed the dog <u>here</u>.

Like adjectives, many adverbs have comparative and superlative forms.

▶ You can make most **comparative adverbs** by adding the suffix *-er*. For longer adverbs, put the word *more* before them. For example: late / later; slowly / more slowly.

▶ You can make most **superlative adverbs** by adding the prefix *-est*. For longer adverbs, put the word *most* before them. For example: late / latest; slowly / most slowly.

Two very common adverb comparatives and superlatives are irregular.

Adverb	Comparative Form	Superlative Form
well	better	best
badly	worse	worst

Placing adverbs can be tricky. In general, you place an adverb before an adjective. (He was <u>hopelessly</u> sad about losing his dog.) But you can place an adverb before a verb, or after it for emphasis. (I <u>slowly</u> washed the dog. I watched <u>helplessly</u> as the dog broke free.) Or you can place it after the object of the verb. (I washed the dog <u>slowly</u>.)

Keywords
- adverbs
- comparative adverbs
- superlative adverbs

*HELPSTER

24

Circumference and Area of a Circle

Circumference (C) is the distance around the outside of a circle. If you put a string around a circle, the length of the string would be the circle's circumference.

Area (A) is the number of square units needed to cover a region. If you know the length of the diameter (*d*) or radius (*r*) of a circle, you can find its area.

To find circumference, use the formula $C = \pi d$.
Use 3.14 for π, which is read "**pi**."

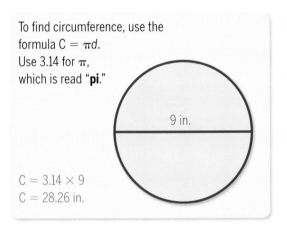

9 in.

$C = 3.14 \times 9$
$C = 28.26$ in.

To find area, use the formula $A = \pi r^2$.
Use 3.14 for π.

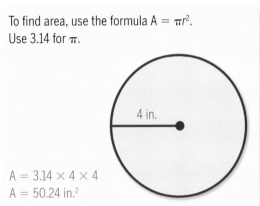

4 in.

$A = 3.14 \times 4 \times 4$
$A = 50.24$ in.^{2}

If you prefer to work with fractions, think of π as $\frac{22}{7}$. 3.14 and $\frac{22}{7}$ are ways we round π to do math. The real π is 3 followed by a decimal that goes on forever! Here's the first part of it: 3.1415926535897 . . .

Keywords
• circumference
• area
• pi

Math

Verbs

A **verb** is a word that tells what a noun does or is. The two main categories of verbs are **action verbs** and **linking verbs**.

▶ Action verbs describe action. Examples: *wash, write, frown, yell, jump, win, eat, stand, draw, hide.* Sample sentence: I <u>wash</u> the dog. (The verb *wash* tells what I do.)

▶ Linking verbs describe a state of being. Examples: *be, seem, feel, look.* Sample sentence: Hank <u>is</u> not a dog lover. (The verb *is* links Hank to a phrase that describes him.)

Regular verbs form their past tense by adding *-d* or *-ed*. **Irregular verbs** form it in other ways. Some very common verbs are irregular.

Verb	Present	Past	Future
be	am / is / are	was / were	will be
have	have / has	had	will have
go	go / goes	went	will go

The following verbs are frequently confused and misused.

Verb	The Difference	Examples
lay / lie	Lay takes an object. Lie does not.	I carefully <u>lay</u> the plates on the table. Do you want to <u>lie</u> down?
raise / rise	Raise takes an object. Rise does not.	<u>Raise</u> your hand if you know the answer. Everyone please <u>rise</u>.

Keywords
- verb
- action verbs
- linking verbs
- regular verbs
- irregular verbs

Symmetry

A figure has **line symmetry** if it can be folded so that both sides match.
The fold itself is called a **line of symmetry**.

How many lines of symmetry do each of these figures have?

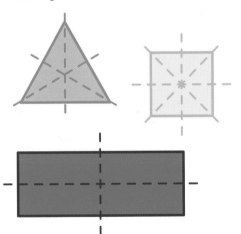

A figure has **rotational symmetry** if it can be rotated less than a full turn around a point and still look exactly the same.

Which of these figures has rotational symmetry?

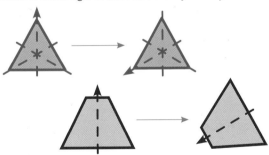

The triangle has rotational symmetry.
The trapezoid does not.

If a figure must be rotated 360° in order to look exactly the same, it does not have rotational symmetry.

Keywords
• line symmetry
• line of symmetry
• rotational symmetry

Math

Adjectives

We have several **colors** to choose from!

Adjectives are words that describe nouns. They answer questions such as "What kind?" or "How many?" about a noun.

▶ What kind? orange, tall, shiny, mean, clean, old

▶ How many? several, few, many, seven, enough

You can use adjectives to compare nouns. To do this, adjectives change form.

▶ **Comparative adjectives** compare two nouns. You can make most comparatives by adding the suffix -er to adjectives. For longer adjectives, put the word *more* before them. Examples: crazy / crazier; fascinating / more fascinating

▶ **Superlative adjectives** compare more than two items. You can make most superlatives by adding the suffix-est to adjectives. For longer adjectives, put the word *most* before them. Examples: crazy / craziest; fascinating / most fascinating

> Notice how the *y* changes to *i* before the ending is added.

Some very common comparatives and superlatives are irregular.

Adjective	Comparative Form	Superlative Form
good (good friend)	better (better friend)	best (best friend)
bad (bad dog)	worse (worse dog)	worst (worst dog)
much or many (many moms)	more (more moms)	most (most moms)

Keywords
- adjectives
- comparative adjectives
- superlative adjectives

✳ HELPSTER

22

Congruence and Similarity

Congruent figures have the same shape and size. The symbol ≅ is used to show that two figures are congruent.

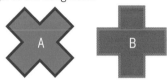

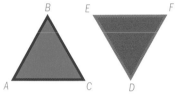

Figure A ≅ Figure B   Triangle *ABC* ≅ Triangle *DEF*

Similar figures have the same shape but may be different sizes. Their **corresponding angles** (e.g., ∠A and ∠D) are the same size, but their corresponding sides (e.g., *AB* and *DE*) can be different lengths. The symbol ∼ is used to show that two figures are similar.

These monsters are similar.   Rectangle E ∼ Rectangle F

A **scale factor** tells you the relationship between the sides of two similar figures. Multiply the length of each side of the smaller shape by the scale factor to find the length of the **corresponding side** in the larger shape.

Keywords
- congruent figures
- similar figures
- corresponding angles
- scale factor
- corresponding side

Math

*HELPSTER

Pronouns

A **pronoun** is a noun that stands in for another noun.
Three common types of pronouns are **subject pronouns**,
object pronouns, and **possessive pronouns**

Pronoun Type	What It Does	Pronouns	Examples
Subject	acts as the subject of a sentence	*I, he, she, it, we, you, they*	Rufus ran away. He ran away. (The noun *Rufus* is replaced by the pronoun *he*.)
Object	acts as the object of a sentence	*me, her, him, it, us, you, them*	I washed Rufus. I washed him. (The noun *Rufus* is replaced by the object pronoun *him*.)
Possessive	shows who owns something	*Mine, hers, his, its, ours, yours, theirs*	That dog is Hank's. That dog is his. (*His* replaces the possessive noun *Hank's*.)

Make sure you use singular pronouns to replace singular nouns and plural pronouns to replace plural nouns. Example: *everyone* is a singular noun.

Keywords
- pronoun
- subject pronouns
- object pronouns
- possessive pronouns

Reflection, Translation, and Rotation

Figures remain congruent when they are reflected, translated, or rotated.

A **reflection** produces a mirror image.

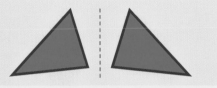

A **translation** moves a figure along a line.

A **rotation** turns a figure around a point.

If a congruent figure moves more than once, it is still congruent. For example: If a congruent figure is rotated, translated, *and* reflected, it remains congruent.

Keywords
- reflection
- translation
- rotation

Math

37

✳HELPSTER

GRAMMAR AND PUNCTUATION
Nouns

Nouns are words that name people, places, things, or ideas.

people	place	thing	idea
Hank	house	shampoo	freedom

You can make most nouns **plural** by adding s to the end of them. For example: dog / dogs. However, some nouns have **irregular plurals**.

Nouns Ending in . . .	How to Make the Plural	Examples
ch, s, sh, x, and z	add -es	bench / benches; bus / buses; dress / dresses; dish / dishes; box / boxes; quiz / quizzes (Here you double the consonant before adding -es.)
f or fe	Say the plural form out loud. If you hear an f sound, add -s to the word. If you hear a v sound, change the f or fe to v. Then add -es.	puff / puffs; giraffe / giraffes; wife / wives
o	If there is a vowel before the o, add -s. If there is a consonant before the o, add -es.	ratio / ratios; hero / heroes
y	If there is a vowel before the y, add -s. If there is a consonant before the y, change y to i. Then add -es.	survey / surveys; penny / pennies

Some nouns form plurals without adding -s: mouse / mice; tooth / teeth; man / men; woman / women; person / people; foot / feet; child / children; ox / oxen. Other nouns, including shrimp, sheep, and deer, don't change at all in the plural.

Keywords
- nouns
- plural
- irregular plurals

HELPSTER

20

Solids

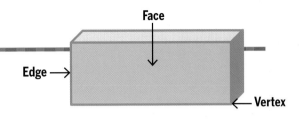

Solid figures are also called **three-dimensional** shapes.
Their three dimensions are length, width, and depth.
Two-dimensional shapes have only length and width.

Face

Edge →

← Vertex

A solid figure is made up of **faces**, **edges**, and **vertices**.

Solid figures can be identified by their number of faces and edges.

Rectangular prism	**Cone**	**Cylinder**	**Sphere**	**Triangular pyramid**
6 faces, 12 edges, 8 vertices	1 flat face, 1 curved surface, 1 edge, 1 vertex	2 flat faces, 1 curved surface, 2 edges, 0 vertices	0 flat faces, 1 curved surface, 0 edges, 0 vertices	4 faces, 6 edges, 4 vertices
(A cube has six equal faces.)				

A **prism** has two congruent bases.
A **pyramid** has only one base.

Keywords
- solid figure
- three-dimensional
- face
- edge
- vertices (vertex)

Math

✳HELPSTER

GRAMMAR AND PUNCTUATION
Capitalization

When should a word or phrase be capitalized? Here are some **capitalization** rules.

Capitalize...	Examples
the first word of a sentence or a quotation.	My vet said, "That dog needs to be trained."
all proper nouns and proper adjectives. This means you should capitalize the names of specific people, places, organizations, historical events, nationalities, and ethnic backgrounds.	Hank Hammond, you are a dog hater! Lots of dogs live on Elm Street. A mutt can't be registered with the American Kennel Club. Did people have dogs during the American Revolution?
acronyms.	NASA ROY G BIV
people's titles or family relationships if they come before a name or are used as a name.	I think Mrs. Patel's dog is beautiful. I hope Dad and Uncle John like Rufus.
the first word in a title and all nouns, pronouns, adjectives, adverbs, and prepositions with five or more letters.	Of Mice and Dogs, a Training Guide "Why Mutts Make the Best Pets" "My Life as a Dog"

Sometimes, words with several meanings are capitalized only in certain instances. *Earth* is often capitalized when the word refers to the planet Earth. When the word *earth* is used to mean soil or land, however, it isn't capitalized. If you're not sure when to capitalize a word, check the dictionary.

Keyword
• capitalization

✳HELPSTER

19

Volume

Volume is the measure of space inside a solid figure. The volume of a figure is measured in cubic units, such as **cubic inches** (in.^{3}), **cubic feet** (ft.^{3}), **cubic centimeters** (cm^3), and **cubic meters** (m^3), and so on.

The volume (V) of this rectangular **prism** can be found by counting the number of cubes that will fit inside it.

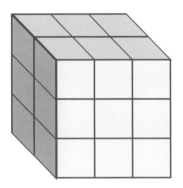

For this prism:
Each layer has 2 rows of 3 cubes.
The prism has 3 layers of cubes.
There are 3 layers of 6 cubes, or 18 cubes.

So V = 18 cubic units or units^3.

Keywords
- volume
- cubic inches
- cubic feet
- cubic centimeters
- cubic meters
- prism
- cylinder

Multiply the area of one of the bases by the height of any prism or **cylinder** to find its volume. The volume of a rectangular prism is: length × width (the area of its base) × height.

Math

39

Colons

Language Arts

A **colon** [:] is a punctuation mark that is used to introduce things. It can introduce a list or series, an example, an explanation, a **quotation**, or a **business letter**.

Use a Colon . . .	Example
to introduce a list or series.	To wash the dog, I needed the following: shampoo, a scrub brush, and a hose.
to introduce an example.	Rufus can get really dirty: Yesterday, he was covered in mud.
to introduce an explanation.	Rufus can get really dirty: He's always running through mud puddles.
to introduce a quotation.	Here's what Hank said about washing the dog: "Washing Rufus is the worst chore ever!"
for the greeting of a business letter.	Dear Sir: I would like some information on your dog obedience school. Sincerely, Hank Hammond
to write time in hours and minutes.	We found Rufus at 6:47 P.M.

Keywords
- colon
- quotation
- business letter
- ratio

In mathematics, a colon can be used to write a **ratio**.
The ratio 4:8 is read "4 to 8."

✳HELPSTER

Surface Area

Surface area is the total area of the surface of a solid figure.
To find the surface area of a solid, first find the area of each **face**.

What is the surface area of this rectangular **prism**?

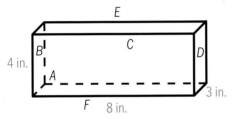

A = Front D = Right side
B = Left side E = Top
C = Back F = Bottom

Look at the six faces of the prism:
A and C are congruent, so they will have the same area.
The same is true of B and D, and E and F.

To find the surface area, you can find the area of each rectangle and add them together, or you can use the formula for the surface area of a rectangular prism:

$SA = 2lw + 2lh + 2wh$
$l = length \; w = width \; h = height$

$SA = 2(8 \text{ in.} \times 3 \text{ in.}) + 2(8 \text{ in.} \times 4 \text{ in.}) + 2(3 \text{ in.} \times 4 \text{ in.})$
$SA = 2(24) + 2(32) + 2(12)$
$SA = 48 + 64 + 24$
$SA = 136 \text{ in.}^2$

When you find the surface area of a solid (or the area of a two-dimensional shape), be sure to write your answer in square units.

Keywords
- surface area
- face
- prism

Math

GRAMMAR AND PUNCTUATION
Apostrophes

An **apostrophe** [**'**] is used for contractions.

Contraction	What the Apostrophe Replaces
<u>I'm</u> going to wash the dog.	the *a* in *am*—I am
Hank <u>doesn't</u> want to help.	the *o* in *not*—does not
<u>We're</u> coming to watch Keisha.	the *a* in *are*—We are

An apostrophe is also used to make **possessive nouns**.

Type of Possessive Noun	How to Add the Apostrophe	Example
singular noun that doesn't end in *s*	add an apostrophe and *s*	The dog's name is Rufus.
singular noun that ends in *s*	add an apostrophe and *s*	Rufus's fur is very dirty.
plural noun that ends in *s*	add only an apostrophe	The dogs' barking is making me crazy.
plural noun that doesn't end in *s*	add an apostrophe and *s*	The children's dogs are all playing.

It's and *they're* are **contractions** that often are confused with similar words. *It's* stands for *it is*. Don't confuse it with *its*, the possessive form of *it*. *They're* stands for *they are*. Don't confuse it with *their*, the possessive form of *they*, or with the adverb *there*.

Keywords
- apostrophe
- possessive nouns
- contractions

Coordinate Grid

A **coordinate grid** uses **ordered pairs** to name points on a graph.

A coordinate grid has four **quadrants** divided by a horizontal line called the **x-axis** and a vertical line called the **y-axis**. The axes and quadrants are labeled on the grid.

What point is located at (3, 2)? ⟶

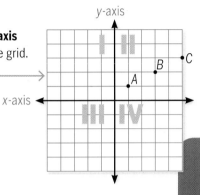

Start at the **origin**, the point where the x-axis meets the y-axis, also known as (0, 0). The first number in an ordered pair tells how many units to move to the right or left. The second number tells how many units to move up or down.

If you move 3 units to the right and 2 units up, you arrive at point *B*.

You can use the **coordinate system** to map shapes onto a grid.

What shape is formed by mapping the following points and connecting them?
(4, 3), (2, −3), (−5, −3), (−3, 3)

The points form a parallelogram.

Keywords
- coordinate grid
- ordered pairs
- quadrants
- x-axis
- y-axis
- origin
- coordinate system

Think of a pair of coordinates as (x, y). If x is a positive number, move right from the origin. If it's negative, move left. If y is a positive integer, move above the origin. If it's negative, move down.

Math

✳HELPSTER

Quotation Marks

Quotation marks[" "] surround what a person says. Anything in quotation marks is an exact record of someone's words. Put quotation marks around only what a person has said. Any other information should be outside the quotation marks.

"That dog always runs away," Hank said.

Exactly what was said   **Who said it.**

▶ In fiction, use quotation marks for **dialogue**. Always start a new paragraph for a new speaker.

▶ Use quotation marks in nonfiction for things people say or for writing you take from another source. Always identify the source of your quotation.

▶ Commas and periods go always inside quotation marks.

▶ Question marks and exclamation points go inside only if they are part of the quote. If they are part of a larger sentence, they go outside the quotation marks.

> Hank asked, "Have you seen this dog?"
> Can you believe Hank said the dog is "a problem"?

Keywords
• quotation marks
• dialogue

Whole Number Patterns

What is the **rule** for this **number pattern**?

> 2, 6, 10, 14, 18, 22 . . .

Each number is 4 more than the one before it.
The rule for this pattern is "add 4."

Some pattern rules have more than one operation.

> 2, 5, 11, 23 . . .

The rule for this pattern is "multiply by 2 and add 1."
What are the fifth and sixth numbers in the pattern?

$23 \times 2 = 46$ $46 + 1 = 47$ $47 \times 2 = 94$ $94 + 1 = 95$

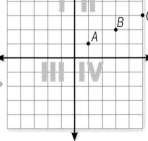

Look at this pattern: ——————————————→
If the pattern continues, what are the coordinates of point D?

Each point increases by $(2, 1)$. $5 + 2 = 7$ $3 + 1 = 4$
So point D will be at $(7, 4)$.

For a rule to be correct, it must work for *every* value in a pattern.
Be sure to check your rule on at least three or four numbers in the pattern.

Keywords
- rule
- number pattern

Math

42

Commas

A **comma** [,] shows a pause in writing or reading. Here are some places to use commas.

Use a Comma . . .	Examples
to set off direct address. (That's when a sentence contains the name of the person to whom it is directed.)	Hank, I already gave the dog a bath. Oh, gosh, Maria, I forgot to do it. Thanks!
after phrases that begin a sentence.	By the way, have you seen the dog? After soaping up the dog, I rinsed him off. Barking loudly, the dog ran away.
to set off interjections.	Uh-oh, that's a huge problem! His disappearance has, well, upset me.
to set off an **appositive**. (An appositive is a noun, pronoun, or phrase that describes or explains another noun or pronoun.)	The dog, a black-and-white mutt, has never run away before. Stray animals, especially dogs, upset me.
between the two independent clauses of a compound sentence.	I'm going to look for the dog, but I have no idea where he might be.

Also use commas to separate items in a list of three or more words. For example:
I will look for the dog at the grocery store, the Porky's Pizza Place, and the bank.

Keywords
• comma
• appositive

HELPSTER

15

ALGEBRA
Geometric Patterns

A **geometric pattern** uses shapes. What is the next shape in this pattern?

The pattern is square, rectangle, triangle. So the next shape will be a rectangle.

A **tessellation** is formed by figures that fit together without overlapping and with no gaps. Tiles on many walls and floors tessellate.

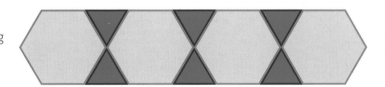

A geometric pattern can also be made with dots.

Each equilateral triangle is formed by adding a number that is one greater than the number that was added to the previous triangle: $3 + 3 = 6; 6 + 4 = 10; 10 + 5 = 15$.

Keywords
• geometric pattern
• tessellation

Math

43

Oxymorons

Has anyone ever told you to "act natural"? If so, they were using an **oxymoron**.

An oxymoron is a **figure of speech** that appears to be a contradiction. The word itself comes from two contradictory Greek roots: *oxys*, "sharp," and *moros*, "foolish." Many oxymorons play on the fact that some words have more than one meaning. Writers use oxymorons because they produce memorable images for readers.

Here are some examples of common oxymorons:

alone together	final draft
almost exactly	open secret
clearly confused	awfully good
sight unseen	loud silence
adult children	far nearer
mutually exclusive	old news
jumbo shrimp	pretty ugly
inside out	found missing
advanced beginner	sad smile

Keywords
- oxymoron
- figure of speech

ALGEBRA
Variables

A **variable** is a letter or symbol that stands for a number. A variable can be used to write an **expression**. An expression is a combination of numbers, variables, or numbers and variables.

Jenna had some storybooks. Jason gave her 5 more.
What expression best represents this? ⟶ $t + 5$

The variable t represents the number of storybooks Jenna had before Jason gave her 5 more.

A variable can be used to write an **equation**. An equation is a math sentence containing an equal sign (=).

After Jason gave Jenna 5 storybooks, she had 16 books. How many books did Jenna have to start with?

$$t + 5 = 16$$
$$16 - 5 = 11, \text{ so } 11 + 5 = 16$$
$$\text{So } t = 11$$

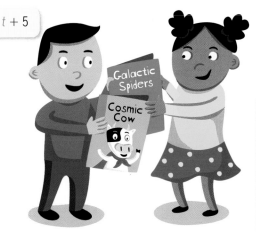

Using **counters** can help you solve an equation.

 $+ t =$

11 counters must be added to the left side of the equation to make both sides equal.
So $t = 11$.

Keywords
- variable
- expression
- equation
- counters

✳HELPSTER

SPELLING AND VOCABULARY
Idioms

An **idiom** is a phrase whose meaning is different from what the words in the phrase literally mean. Idioms, like metaphors and similes, are called **figures of speech** because they create images in the mind. In fact, many idioms are **metaphors**. They imply a comparison between two unlike things.

For example, *going out on a limb* means *taking a risk*. The idiom is a metaphor because it implies a comparison between a risk someone takes and the literal risk of being out on the limb of a tree.

Here are some idioms and their meanings. ⟶

Idiom	Meaning
in the doghouse	in trouble
over the hill	old
break a leg	good luck
spitting image	looks exactly like
off the hook	free from a difficult situation
lion's share	the biggest share
blow your top	get really angry
walking on air	very happy
keep it under your hat	keep it a secret

Why use idioms? They add imagery to writing. Also, people use idioms when they talk, so good writers often use them to make their writing sound more natural.

Keywords
- idiom
- figures of speech
- metaphors

Commutative, Associative, and Distributive Properties

Commutative Property of Addition The order of the addends does not change the sum.	$5 + 8 = 8 + 5$
Commutative Property of Multiplication The order of the factors does not change the product.	$10 \times 12 = 12 \times 10$
Associative Property of Addition The grouping of the addends does not change the sum.	$(7 + 15) + 8 = 7 + (15 + 8)$
Associative Property of Multiplication The grouping of the factors does not change the product.	$(9 \times 6) \times 5 = 9 \times (6 \times 5)$
Distributive Property of Multiplication Multiplying a sum by a number is the same as multiplying each addend by the number.	$38 \times 4 = (30 \times 4) + (8 \times 4)$

The distributive property can help you solve problems mentally. $54 \times 6 = ?$
You know that $50 \times 6 = 300$. You know that $4 \times 6 = 24$.
You can easily add the two products in your head: $300 + 24 = 324$.
So $54 \times 6 = 324$.

Keywords
- Commutative Property
- Associative Property
- Distributive Property

Math

Abbreviations

Abbreviations are short ways of writing words and phrases. There are two kinds of abbreviations.

1. Shortened Words, Names, and People's Titles: These take a period at the end.

Avenue	→ Ave.	Governor	→ Gov.
Company	→ Co.	Incorporated	→ Inc.
Department	→ Dept.	Mister	→ Mr.
government	→ govt.	singular	→ sing.

2. Initials That Stand for the Names of Places, Things, or Organizations: These do not use punctuation. Often, the initials of very short words in the name are not used. These types of abbreviations are also known as **initializations**.

American Broadcasting Corporation	→ ABC
automated teller machine	→ ATM
Colorado Department of Transportation	→ CDOT
United States of America	→ USA
Women's National Basketball Association	→ WNBA

Each U.S. state and territory has a two-letter postal code that does not use periods. For example: AL, Alabama; AR, Arkansas; CA, California; MI, Michigan; TX, Texas.

Keywords
• abbreviations
• initializations

Functions

A **function** is a relationship in which one quantity depends on another quantity. What function is represented by this **function table**?

x	y
2	7
3	8
4	9
5	10

Look at the relationship between the values of x and y. Each y-value is 5 more than its corresponding x-value.

$y = x + 5$

You can graph a function by using the x- and y-values as ordered pairs.

The graph of the function $y = x + 5$ looks like this: ⟶

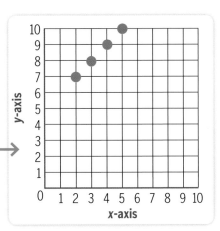

Check if the numbers increase or decrease in a function table. If all the y-values increase compared to the x-values, the function involves addition or multiplication. If the numbers decrease, the function involves subtraction or division.

Keywords
• function
• function table

Math

✕HELPSTER

Homonyms: Homographs

Homographs are words that are spelled alike but have different meanings. English has hundreds of homographs. Sometimes homographs are pronounced differently even though they are spelled the same. Homographs are also known as multiple-meaning words. Here are some examples.

Homograph	Meaning 1	Meaning 2
duck	The duck sat silently on the pond.	You need to duck because the doorway is low.
desert*	Don't desert me here where I don't know anyone.	The desert was beautiful in its stark emptiness.
pitcher	The pitcher of water is on the table.	The pitcher threw a fastball and the batter swung.
moped*	She was sad and moped around the house for days.	When I get older, I'll be able to ride a moped to school.
pupil	The pupil listened closely to the teacher.	The pupil of his left eye looked enlarged.
lean	You can lean on me if you are tired.	The man was lean and muscled from working hard.
present*	I got my brother the greatest birthday present.	Remember that we have to present the class gift today.

* These homographs are pronounced differently.

In Greek, *homo* means "the same" and *graph* means "write." So homographs are two words that are "written (spelled) the same."

Keyword
• homographs

⚹HELPSTER

11

Rates of Change

You can use a **proportion** to express a **constant rate of change**.

Mr. Edwards drove 100 miles in 2 hours. If he drives at the same rate, how far will he go in 4 hours?

Write a proportion: $\frac{100 \text{ miles}}{2 \text{ hours}} = \frac{x \text{ miles}}{4 \text{ hours}}$

Find the **cross products**: $100 \times 4 = 2x$
$400 = 2x$

Divide both sides of the equation by 2: $400 \div 2 = 2x \div 2$
$200 = x$

So in 4 hours he'll drive 200 miles.

Ben collects shells on the beach. Each day, he collects 2 more shells than the day before. This situation represents a **variable rate of change**. It can be shown with a table. ⟶

Day	Shells Collected That Day	Total Shells
1	3	3
2	5	8
3	7	15
4	9	24
5	11	35
6	13	48

Rates of change can be shown on a graph. To graph Mr. Edwards's driving progress, plot the hours and distance as x and y coordinates.

For example: After two hours, he's driven 100 miles. So that point on the grid is represented by the ordered pair (2, 100). What would the other points be?

Keywords
• proportion
• constant rate of change
• cross products
• variable rate of change

Math

47

✳HELPSTER

SPELLING AND VOCABULARY
Homonyms: Homophones

Homonyms are words that are similar in some way. There are two types of homonyms: **homophones** and **homographs**.

Homophones are words that sound alike but have different spellings and different meanings. There are hundreds of homophones in English. Here are some examples.

Homophones	Example 1	Example 2
hoarse / horse	My voice is <u>hoarse</u> from yelling at the game.	A rancher should know how to ride a <u>horse</u>.
aloud / allowed	I love it when someone reads <u>aloud</u> to me.	I'm not <u>allowed</u> to watch TV while doing my homework.
bald / bawled	Many men go <u>bald</u> when they get older.	My brother <u>bawled</u> like a baby after he fell.
blew / blue	A cold wind <u>blew</u> through the stands at the football game.	The team wore red, white, and <u>blue</u> uniforms.
flair / flare	He is successful because he has a <u>flair</u> for business.	The policeman lit a <u>flare</u> next to the disabled car.
guest / guessed	We have a <u>guest</u> staying at our house.	I <u>guessed</u> the answer immediately.
overdo / overdue	Don't <u>overdo</u> your workout or you'll be tired tomorrow.	Those library books are long <u>overdue</u>.

In Greek, *homo* means "the same" and *phone* means "sound." So homophones are two words that "sound the same."

Keywords
- homonyms
- homophones
- homographs

✳HELPSTER

Surveys

A **survey** can be used to collect **data**. A survey might ask all the fifth-grade students to name their favorite animal at the zoo. The results can be displayed in a table.

Animal	Number of Votes
Lion	6
Monkey	10
Zebra	8
Panda	12

This data can also be displayed on a **bar graph**.

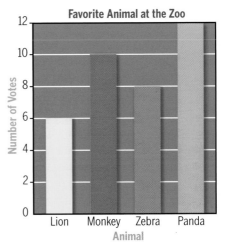

By looking at this graph, you can easily see that the panda got the most votes.

You can use a graph to compare data. How many more votes did the monkey get than the lion? By comparing the bars in the graph, you can see that the monkey got 4 more votes than the lion.

Keywords
• survey
• data
• bar graph

Math

48

✳HELPSTER

Compound Words

A **compound word** combines two smaller words. Take a look at these compound words.

break + fast = breakfast	flash+ light = flashlight
eye + witness = eyewitness	grand + daughter = granddaughter
back + ground = background	light + hearted = lighthearted
butter + fly = butterfly	motor + cycle = motorcycle
earth + quake = earthquake	school + teacher = schoolteacher

To figure out the meaning of a compound word, first break it into its two shorter words. Think about the meaning of each smaller word. Then think about how those meanings could fit together. For instance, the noun *eye* is "an organ used to see" and *witness* is "someone who observes what happens during an event." So an *eyewitness* "sees what happens during an event."

Sometimes, the meaning of a compound word can't be figured out from the words in it. Is a *butterfly* a "fly made of butter"? If the two shorter words don't make sense together, try to define the compound word from the context. Or look it up in a dictionary.

Keyword
• compound word

✳HELPSTER

Comparing Bar Graphs and Line Graphs

A **bar graph** is useful for comparing different amounts. This graph shows club membership. Which club has the most members?

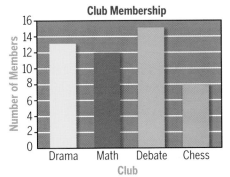

Club Membership

The bar for the debate club is the tallest, so it has the most members.

A **line graph** is best for showing how data changes over time. How did the temperature change according to this graph?

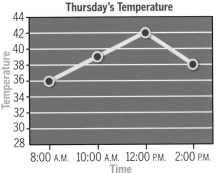

Thursday's Temperature

By looking at this graph, you can see that the temperature rose and then fell.

Both of the graphs shown here have intervals of 2 on the vertical axis. If the data falls between these intervals of 2, it has the value halfway between those two intervals. So the temperature at 10:00 A.M. was 39°F.

Keywords
• bar graph
• line graph

Math

49

Acronyms

Acronyms are several first initials put together and pronounced as a word. Acronyms usually represent the name of an organization, like NASA (National Aeronautics and Space Administration). They can also represent the first letters of a group of words that need to be remembered together.

There are four rules to remember when writing acronyms:

▶ Acronyms are written in all capital letters.

▶ There are no periods between the capital letters of an acronym.

▶ Small words like *the* and *of* are not usually represented in an acronym.

▶ Acronyms are pronounced like words and not as separate letters.

Here are some common acronyms:

▶ **NASA**: **N**ational **A**eronautics and **S**pace **A**dministration

▶ **SCUBA**: **s**elf-**c**ontained **u**nderwater **b**reathing **a**pparatus

▶ **MADD**: **M**others **A**gainst **D**runk **D**riving

▶ **ROY G BIV**: The colors of the rainbow, in order: **r**ed, **o**range, **y**ellow, **g**reen, **b**lue, **i**ndigo, **v**iolet

Some acronyms, like *scuba* and *laser*, have become words in English and are no longer written only in capital letters. (Laser stands for **l**ight **a**mplification by **s**timulated **e**mission of **r**adiation.)

Keyword
• acronyms

*HELPSTER

8

Histograms and Circle Graphs

A **histogram** is a bar graph that shows the occurrence of data within intervals.

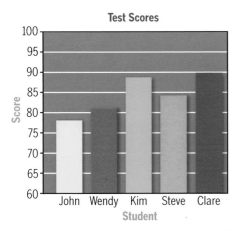

Test Scores

On this test, most students scored between 81 and 90.

A **circle graph** shows parts of a whole. This graph shows how Sasha spends her free time. What does she spend the least amount of time doing?

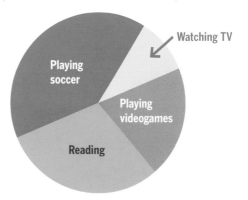

The smallest section of the graph is Watching TV, so this is the activity that Sasha spends the least amount of time doing.

In a histogram, the intervals on the horizontal axis must be equal and must not overlap.

Keywords
• histogram
• circle graph

Math

50

Synonyms and Antonyms

Synonyms are words that have the same, or nearly the same, meanings. Here are some pairs of synonyms.

happy / glad	fast / rapid
smart / intelligent	terrible / horrible
similar / alike	wonderful / great
disease / sickness	angry / mad
journey / voyage	unhappy / sad
pretty / beautiful	amazing / incredible
locate / find	walk / stroll
big / large	alone / solitary
liberty / freedom	friend / pal

To choose a synonym for a word, ask: Which word has the same, or nearly the same, meaning?

Antonyms are words that have opposite, or nearly opposite, meanings. Here are some pairs of antonyms.

happy / sad	courteous / impolite
tall / short	terrible / wonderful
similar / unlike	heavy / light
disease / health	love / hate
pretty / ugly	build / destroy
believe / doubt	empty / crowded
big / little	empty / full
fast / slow	hungry / full
work / play	dry / wet

To choose an antonym for a word, ask: Which word has the opposite, or nearly the opposite, meaning?

Keywords
• synonyms
• antonyms

Range, Median, Mean, and Mode

There are several ways to analyze data. Here is an example of a **data set**:

32, 19, 21, 25, 31, 29, 25

▶ The **range** of a data set is the difference between the greatest number and the least number. Here, the greatest number is 32. The least number is 19.

$32 - 19 = \textbf{13}$
So the range is 13.

▶ The **median** is the middle number, when the numbers are ordered from least to greatest.

19, 21, 25, **25**, 29, 31, 32
So the median is 25.

▶ The **mean** is found by adding the numbers in the data set and dividing by the number of addends. $32 + 19 + 21 + 25 + 31 + 29 + 25 = 182$

$182 \div 7 = \textbf{26}$
So the mean is 26.

▶ The **mode** is the number that occurs most often. 25 is the only number that appears more than once.

So the mode is 25.

To find the median when there is an even number of data, find the mean of the middle two numbers.

Keywords
- data set
- range
- median
- mean
- mode

Math

51

✳HELPSTER

Here are some examples of Greek and Latin prefixes and suffixes.

Prefix	Meaning	Origin
auto-	self	Greek
bi-	two	Latin
contra-, contro-	against	Latin
hemi-	half	Greek
idea-, ideo-	idea	Greek
inter-	between	Latin
micro-	small	Greek
trans-	over, across	Latin

Suffix	Meaning	Origin
-ant	thing or person	Latin
-ent	to form	Latin
-ial	in the manner of	Latin
-ic	has the quality of	Greek & Latin
-ism	act or process of	Greek & Latin
-ize	to become like	Latin
-fy	make or do	Latin
-logy	the study of	Greek

Language Arts

Use the charts to figure out the meanings of these words:
1. controversial   2. bicentennial   3. microbiology

Keywords
• base words
• prefixes
• suffixes

HELPSTER

6

Ratios and Proportion

A **ratio** is a comparison of two quantities. A ratio can compare a part to a part or a part to a whole.

What is the ratio of moons to suns?

A ratio can be written three ways: 3 to 6, 3:6, or $\frac{3}{6}$.

A ratio can also be written in simplest form: $\frac{3}{6} = \frac{1}{2}$.

Now, what is the ratio of moons to *all* the shapes?
The number of moons = 3.
The total number of shapes = 9.
So the ratio is 3 to 9, 3:9, or $\frac{3}{9}$. In simplest form: $\frac{1}{3}$.

A **proportion** shows that two ratios are equal.

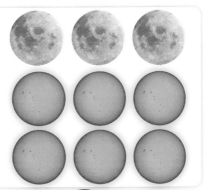

Carol read 5 books in 3 months. At the same rate, how many books will she read in 9 months?

Write a proportion: $\frac{5}{3} = \frac{n}{9}$

Find the cross products: $3n = 5 \times 9$ $3n = 45$

Solve for *n*: $3n \div 3 = 45 \div 3$ $n = 15$

You can find out if two ratios make a proportion by finding the cross products. If the cross products are equal, the ratios make a proportion.

Keywords
• ratio
• proportion

Math

✳HELPSTER

Word Origins

Many English words and word parts come from other languages, particularly Greek and Latin. **Base words**, **prefixes**, and **suffixes** can all come from Greek or Latin words. Knowing these roots and their meanings can help you to figure out the meaning of an unknown word.

Look at these charts of Greek and Latin base words. Then turn the page to find some prefixes and suffixes.

Base Word	Meaning	Origin	Example
bio	life	Greek	biography
cent	one hundred	Latin	century
cred	believe, trust	Latin	credible
dict	say or speak	Latin	diction
gram, graph	write, draw, record	Greek	telegram
photo	light	Greek	photograph
scrib, script	to write	Latin	transcribe
vers, vert	to turn	Latin	inverse

What Is Probability?

Probability is the chance that an event will happen.

Suppose you closed your eyes and picked a marble from this group:

▶ An event that is **certain** must happen. It is certain you'll pick a marble that is not yellow.

▶ A **likely** event will probably happen. It is likely that you'll pick a black marble.

▶ An **unlikely** event will probably not happen. It is unlikely that you'll pick a white marble.

▶ An **impossible** event can't happen. It's impossible that you'll pick a striped marble.

Events that are **equally likely** have the same chance of happening. If you spin this spinner, the chances of spinning a 1 or a 4 are equally likely.

An event that is certain has a probability of 1.
An event that is impossible has a probability of 0.

Keywords
- probability
- certain
- likely
- unlikely
- impossible
- equally likely

Math

53

▶ **Explanation or Description Clues**: See if anything near the word explains or describes it.

Americans are very fond of their **vehicles**. The four wheels, the gleaming metal, the roaring engine, and the cozy interior all have a special place in an owner's heart.

> The context clue describes the word *vehicle*.

▶ **Antonym or Contrast Clues**: Look for a word or phrase that contrasts with the unknown word or is its **antonym**. These clues are often introduced with the words *in contrast to*, *however*, *but*, or *instead of*.

Suburban Americans use their **vehicles** a lot. In contrast, city dwellers tend to walk more.

> The context clue contrasts walking with using *vehicles*, so it's a clue to that word's meaning.

If you come to an unfamiliar word in a book and context clues don't help, see if the word is in the book's glossary. Or look up the term in the book's index to find out where else it is used. Perhaps it's illustrated or defined on another page.

Keywords
- synonym
- context clues
- antonym
- contrast clues

✳HELPSTER

4

Tree Diagrams and Probability

You can use a **tree diagram** to show all the **possible outcomes** of a situation.
Suppose you have 3 shirts and 4 pairs of pants.
How many different outfits can you make?

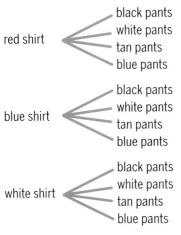

	black pants	red shirt/black pants
red shirt	white pants	red shirt/white pants
	tan pants	red shirt/tan pants
	blue pants	red shirt/blue pants

	black pants	blue shirt/black pants
blue shirt	white pants	blue shirt/white pants
	tan pants	blue shirt/tan pants
	blue pants	blue shirt/blue pants

	black pants	white shirt/black pants
white shirt	white pants	white shirt/white pants
	tan pants	white shirt/tan pants
	blue pants	white shirt/blue pants

The tree diagram shows you that there are 12 possible outfits.

Find the probability of picking an outfit with a white shirt:
The tree diagram shows 12 choices in all. There are 4 choices with a white shirt.
So the probability of picking an outfit with a white shirt is $\frac{4}{12}$, or $\frac{1}{3}$.

Keywords
• tree diagram
• possible outcomes

Math

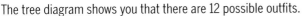

54

Context Clues

Sometimes, you'll come across an unknown word in your reading. You can look at the words around the unknown word for help. These words are called **context clues.** Here are some types of context clues.

▶ **Definition or Synonym Clues**: A definition or a **synonym** for the word may be nearby. Look for it.

Vehicles, or cars, are a popular way to get around.

> The context clue *cars* is a synonym for the word *vehicles*.

▶ **Example Clues**: See if there are any examples that hint at the word's meaning. Examples are often introduced with the words *like, such as, include* or *including,* or *for example*.

Most Americans own at least one **vehicle**, such as a car, a truck, or an SUV.

> The context clue gives examples that point to the meaning of the word *vehicle*.

Understanding the Problem

There are strategies you can use to help you understand and solve a **word problem**.

> Ellen is packing fruit into boxes. She has 20 pieces of fruit and 3 boxes. There are 15 apples and 5 oranges. She wants to put 6 pieces of fruit in each box. How many pieces of fruit will be left over?

Sometimes a problem contains information that's not necessary to solve it. It's helpful to cross out irrelevant information and underline the key information.

> Ellen is packing fruit into boxes. <u>She has 20 pieces of fruit</u> and <u>3 boxes</u>. ~~There are 15 apples and 5 oranges.~~ She wants to put <u>6 pieces of fruit in each box</u>. How many pieces of fruit will be left over?

You can use a drawing to help you understand the problem.

Each circle represents a piece of fruit. After the boxes are full, keep drawing until there are 20 pieces of fruit. There are 2 left over.

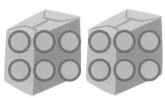

When solving a word problem, make sure you correctly identify the question that is being asked.

Keywords
- word problem
- irrelevant information
- key information

Math

SPELLING AND VOCABULARY
Using a Dictionary

Dictionaries are very useful reference tools. They can help you spell or define any word. Here's what you'll find in a typical **dictionary** entry.

This is the **entry word**. The entry word is the word about which information is being given. Entry words are broken into their syllables. Often, dictionaries will have only one form of a word as an entry word. So if you are looking for *studiously*, check *studious*.

The spelling in parentheses tells you how the word should be pronounced.

stu•di•ous (**stoo**-dee-uhss)

adjective [from the Latin *studium*—eagerness]

This is the **etymology**. An etymology tells you a word's history.

1. given to studying very hard.
2. given a steady and careful effort. **3.** deliberate.

noun: **studiousness**; adverb: **studiously**

This tells you what part of speech the word is.

This is the **definition**. For words with more than one meaning, more than one definition is given. Each one is numbered. Look for the definition that works best in each situation.

Dictionaries are organized alphabetically. Use the two **guide words** at the top of a dictionary page to determine if your word is on that page. If the spelling of your word falls between a page's guide words, your word should be on that page.

Keywords
- dictionary
- entry word
- etymology
- definition
- guide words

Estimating

Sometimes you only need to estimate to answer a problem. An **estimate** is an answer that is close to the exact answer. One way to estimate is by **rounding**.

Felix has $20.00 to spend at the bookstore. He wants to buy a science fiction book for $5.99, a mystery for $7.45, and a birthday card for $2.89. Does he have enough money?

Round up each number and add:

$5.99 → $6.00	$6.00	
$7.45 → $8.00	$8.00	
$2.89 → $3.00	+$3.00	
	$17.00	$17.00 < $20.00, so Felix has enough money.

If Felix wants to know how much change he will get back,
an estimate will not be enough. He will need an exact answer.

Sometimes rounding to a lesser place will give you a more precise estimate:

Rounding to the thousands place	Rounding to the hundreds place	Exact answer
1,263 → 1,000	1,263 → 1,300	1,263
2,519 → 3,000	2,519 → 2,500	2,519
+4,860 → +5,000	+4,860 → +4,900	+4,860
9,000	8,700	8,642

Keywords
- estimate
- rounding

Math

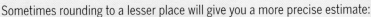

SPELLING AND VOCABULARY
Spelling Words Correctly

Not all words in the English language are spelled the way they sound. And some sounds can be spelled with a number of different letter combinations. So, how can you be sure to spell a word correctly? Here are four steps to follow.

Look for the Word in Print	Sound It Out	Use a Dictionary	Use a Spell-Checker
Think about places you might find the word already written. Is it on your assignment sheet? Is it in a book you're using?	Sounding out a word can help you spell it. Break the word into **syllables**. Then try sounding out and spelling each syllable.	If you're still not sure how to spell a word, look it up in a **dictionary**. The dictionary will give you the correct spelling every time.	You can use a computer **spell-checker** instead of a dictionary. Open a document. Then type the word as you think it might be spelled. Run the spell-checker to find out if you're right. But note that proper nouns, foreign words, and uncommon words may not be in your spell-checker, and it can't show you which homonym to use. A dictionary is a better source for those words.

Always reread what you write and check any words you think might be misspelled. Even do it in e-mails. Fixing spelling mistakes guarantees that readers will get your message loud and clear.

Keywords
• syllable
• dictionary
• spell-checker

✳HELPSTER

Solving Two-Step Word Problems

It may take two or more steps to solve a word problem.
In this case, break the problem into smaller parts in order to solve it.

> Carly earned $15.00 babysitting, $19.50 helping her mother at the office,
> and $12.00 helping her neighbor with yard work. She wants to save $55.00
> for a new pair of sneakers. How much more money does Carly need
> to reach her goal?

This problem has two steps:

1. Find how much money Carly has already earned by adding.

$$\begin{array}{r} \$15.00 \\ \$19.50 \\ +\ \$12.00 \\ \hline \$46.50 \end{array}$$

2. Now find how much money she still needs to earn by subtracting.

$$\begin{array}{r} \$55.00 \\ -\ \$46.50 \\ \hline \$8.50 \end{array}$$

Look for key words to decide which steps to use.
In the example above, "how much more" tells you to use subtraction.

Keywords
• two-step problem

Math

✳HELPSTER

Language Arts **Keywords** (continued)

Showing Your Work

Sometimes you will be asked to **show your work** and explain how you got your answer.

Stephen finished 12 of the 15 books on his summer reading list.
What percent of the books on the list did Stephen read?

You can use words and numbers to show your work and explain your answer:

First write a fraction to represent the situation:

12 books read out of 15 total books = $\frac{12}{15}$.

Then, convert the fraction to a decimal.
To do this, divide the numerator by the denominator:

$$15\overline{)12.0}^{\,0.8}$$

Now convert the decimal to a percent by multiplying by 100:

$$100 \times 0.8 = 80\%$$

So Stephen read 80% of the books on his list.

You can also explain your reasoning with charts, graphs, tables, or diagrams.
Showing your work always helps you understand the problem better, and can help
you catch errors in your thinking.

Keywords
• show your work

Math

58

Language Arts **Keywords**

Checking Your Work

One way to check your work is to decide if your answer is **reasonable**. Kathleen and Marty both solved the same problem and got different answers.

Estimate to see which answer is reasonable.
5,000 × 20 = 100,000
100,000 is close to 105,800, so Kathleen's answer is reasonable.

You can also use **inverse operations** to check your work. Kathleen solved this problem:

$$\begin{array}{r} 1,219 \\ + \ 546 \\ \hline 1,765 \end{array}$$

Addition and subtraction are inverse operations, so Kathleen can use subtraction to check her answer.

$$\begin{array}{r} 1,765 \\ - \ 546 \\ \hline 1,219 \end{array}$$

Her answer is correct.

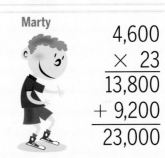

Kathleen

$$\begin{array}{r} 4,600 \\ \times \quad 23 \\ \hline 13,800 \\ + \ 92,000 \\ \hline 105,800 \end{array}$$

Marty

$$\begin{array}{r} 4,600 \\ \times \quad 23 \\ \hline 13,800 \\ + \ 9,200 \\ \hline 23,000 \end{array}$$

If a question has more than one part, make sure you have answered all parts of the question. This is an important part of checking your work.

Keywords
• reasonable
• estimate
• inverse operations

Math

HELPSTER

Language Arts Contents (continued)

Way to go!

Cats Are BETTER! by Julie Smith

Notes

Language Arts Contents

Rufus

Copyright © 2007 by Play Bac Publishing USA, Inc.

All rights reserved. No portion of this book may be reproduced mechanically, electronically, or by any other means, including photocopying, without written permission of the publisher.

ISBN-13: 978-1-60214-002-8

Play Bac Publishing USA, Inc.
225 Varick Street
New York, NY 10014-4381

Printed in China

Distributed by
Black Dog & Leventhal Publishers, Inc.
151 West 19th Street
New York, NY 10011

First printing, January 2007

Play Bac Publishing wishes to thank all the teachers, mothers, and children who have helped develop the books in the Helpster series.

SPECIAL THANKS to: Anne Burrus, Catherine Rupf, Sue Macy, Gramercy Books Service, Steve Tomecek, Susan Buckley, Sunita Apte, Justine Henning, Joan L. Giurdanella, Joe and Denise Kiernan, and the great team at the Bill SMITH STUDIO.

All the books in the Play Bac series have been tested by families and teachers and edited and proofread by professionals in the field.

Please send your comments to:
Play Bac Publishing
225 Varick Street
New York, NY 10014-4381

Thanks!